Boa Constrictors

Boa Constrictor Comprehens

Boa Constrictor Care, behavior, enclosures, feeding, health, myths and interaction all included.

by

Marvin Murkett and Ben Team

ALL RIGHTS RESERVED. This book contains material protected under International and Federal Copyright Laws and Treaties.

Any unauthorized reprint or use of this material is strictly prohibited. No part of this book may be reproduced or transmitted in any form or by any means, electronic, mechanical or otherwise, including photocopying or recording, or by any information storage and retrieval system without express written permission from the author.

Copyrighted © 2015

Published by: IMB Publishing

Table of Contents

Table of Contents

About The Authors 7

Foreword 8

Chapter 1: Boa Constrictor Basics 12
   1) Description and Anatomy 12
   2) Biology 20
   3) Behavior 23
   4) Reproductive Behavior and Biology 25

Chapter 2: Classification and Taxonomy 27

Chapter 3: The Boa Constrictor's World 29
   1) Range 29
   2) Habitat 30
   3) Natural Diet 31
   4) Natural Predators 31
   5) Other Sources of Mortality 32

Chapter 4: The Boa Constrictor as a Pet 33
   1) Understanding the Commitment 33
   2) The Costs of Captivity 34
   3) Myths and Misunderstandings 38
   4) Acquisition and Selection 40
   5) Acquiring Your Boa 42
   6) Quarantine 43

Chapter 5: Providing the Captive Habitat 45
   1) Enclosure ....
   2) Temperature ....

Table of Contents

   3) Thermal Gradients 50

   4) Heat Lamps 51

   5) Ceramic Heat Emitters 52

   6) Radiant Heat Panels 53

   7) Heat Pads 54

   8) Heat Tape 54

   9) Heat Cables 55

   10) Hot Rocks 55

   11) Thermometers 56

   12) Thermostats and Rheostats 57

   13) Nighttime Heating 60

   14) Incorporating Thermal Mass 60

   15) Room Heat 61

   16) Lights 62

   17) Security 62

   18) Substrate 63

   19) Cage Furniture 66

   20) Hide Boxes 67

   21) Humid Hides 69

   22) A Final Word about the Importance of Hides 70

   23) Climbing Branches 70

Chapter 6: Maintaining the Captive Habitat 75

   1) Cleaning Procedures 75

   2) Chemicals & Tools 76

   3) Keeping Records 78

Chapter 7: Feeding Captive Boa Constrictors 82

   1) Live, Fresh Killed or Frozen 82

   2) Prey Species 82

Table of Contents

    3) Prey Size 83

    4) How to Offer Food 83

    5) Problem Feeders 85

    6) Feeding Frequency 85

    7) Avoiding Regurgitation 86

Chapter 8: Boa Constrictor Hydration 87

    1) Humidity 87

    2) Misting 88

    3) Drinking Water 88

    4) Soaking Water 89

    5) Common Husbandry Problems and Solutions 90

Chapter 9: Interacting with Pet Boa Constrictors 93

    1) Handling 93

    2) Picking up a Snake 93

    3) How to Hold a Snake 94

    4) Safely Handling Large Boas 94

    5) Dealing with Aggressive Snakes 95

    6) In The Event of a Bite 96

    7) Temporary Transport Cages 96

    8) Transporting Tips 97

    9) Hygiene 97

Chapter 10: Common Health Concerns 98

    1) Finding a Suitable Veterinarian 98

    2) Reasons to Visit the Veterinarian 99

    3) Common Health Problems 100

Chapter 11: Color Variations 107

    1) Patterns of Inheritance 107

Table of Contents

   2) Color Mutations 109

   3) Pattern Mutations 110

   4) Mutation Combinations 112

Chapter 12: Breeding Boa Constrictors 114

   1) Determining Gender 114

   2) Pre-Breeding Considerations 114

   3) Pre-Breeding Conditioning 115

   4) Cycling 115

   5) Pairing 116

   6) Eliciting Copulation 116

   7) Gestation 117

   8) Parturition 117

   9) Neonatal Husbandry 118

Chapter 13: Selected Subspecies Accounts 119

   1) Common Boas (Boa constrictor imperator) 119

   2) Red-tailed Boas (Boa constrictor constrictor) 120

   3) Argentine Boas (Boa constrictor occidentalis) 121

   4) Long-tailed Boa (Boa constrictor longicauda) 122

   5) Hog Island Boas (Boa constrictor imperator) 122

   6) "Dwarf" Boas 123

Chapter 14: Further Reading 125

References 131

Index 133

About The Authors

Marvin Murkett is an experienced writer and a true animal lover. He has been keeping reptiles and amphibians for over 30 years. He enjoys writing animal books and advising others how to take care of their animals to give them a happy home.

Ben Team is an environmental educator and author with over 16 years of professional reptile-keeping experience.

Ben currently maintains www.FootstepsInTheForest.com, where he shares information, narration and observations of the flora, fauna and habitats of Metro Atlanta.

While he thoroughly enjoys writing about the natural world, Ben's favorite moments are those spent in the company of his beautiful wife.

Foreword

Few ambassadors of the wild are as iconic as the boa constrictor. Silent, stealthy and strong, boas epitomize the idea a tropical forest predator. Clad in handsome colors and reaching up to 50 pounds or more in weight, boa constrictors are striking animals that leave a strong impression on all who observe them. It should come as no surprise that they are popular among snake enthusiasts.

Viewing or handling a boa is a transcendental experience that transports the observer to a far off place, where humans are only visitors. Keeping one as a pet allows you to bring part of this far off land into your living room. But, as with any endeavor worth doing, this is much easier said than done.

While most boas become fine captives and suitable pets for those with the necessary dedication, skills and resources, they are not suitable for everyone. Boas are animals that command respect.

Important: Equipped with unthinkably strong muscles and a mouth full of sharp teeth, boas are capable of causing severe wounds. While serious injuries are rare, the potential for them is real. Boas are not suitable pets for children. Boas are also not suitable pets for adults who don't give their boa the proper care.

Like all wild animals, boas require a more significant level of care than domestic animals, such as dogs and cats do. Domestic animals have been bred to live alongside humans, which greatly reduces the level of care they require. For wild animals, you must take over the job of Mother Nature and provide the resources necessary for your pet to survive. This may require you to learn more about biology, physics, geography and other subjects to provide a quality environment for your pet.

The first step for devising a successful boa constrictor husbandry protocol is to understand the lives and needs of wild boa constrictors. Then, by combining this knowledge with the teachings of more experienced keepers, hobbyists can begin to distinguish between those aspects of the wild that are necessary for their pet's well-being and survival, and which ones are best discarded.

For example, wild boa constrictors crawl alongside monkeys, jaguars and giant fig trees, yet such items are certainly not appropriate to include in your pet boa's cage. Similarly, wild boas derive significant benefits from the leaf litter substrate they live on, but captive boas thrive when kept on a simple paper substrate.

Some considerations have little bearing on the ability of a pet boa to survive, but they may improve the animal's quality of life. Climbing branches, for instance, are not necessary for proper maintenance, but most boas – particularly young or small animals – use them when provided.

Further enhancing their wild nature, snakes are infamous for their ability to capture, kill and consume live rodents and birds. For some, the idea of feeding such prey to their snake is a significant component of the desire to keep a pet snake in the first place; for others, it is so distasteful that it prevents them from keeping snakes at all. While it is true that boa constrictors require whole-food items for sustenance, most will consume prey whether it is alive or dead. In fact, this is true of most healthy, captive snakes. Most keepers can and should feed their snakes pre-killed food items. Doing so provides the snake with a safer meal, and affords the prey animal a more humane death. Additionally, pre-killed rodents are far more convenient for keepers, most of whom can simply purchase frozen rodents from their local pet store as needed.

Foreword

Veterinarian care is important for all animals, and snakes are no different. Because their biology is fundamentally different from that of dogs or cats, you must find a veterinarian that understands their physiology, husbandry and, to some extent, their natural history. Fortunately, snakes do not require vaccinations or other preventative care, and their hardy constitution helps them to remain healthy when provided with sound husbandry. Nevertheless, husbandry mistakes happen and some boas fall sick to diseases that have nothing to do with their husbandry. At such times, a veterinarian who is knowledgeable about snakes is worth his or her weight in gold.

The 21st century boa enthusiasts are quite lucky. Until the 1980s, those who wanted a pet boa were limited to stressed, parasitized animals that had been plucked directly from their rainforest homes. Currently, captive bred boas are more readily available to hobbyists than wild caught animals are. Such captive bred animals make far better pets than their wild-caught ancestors did. These captive bred offspring are usually hardy and healthy, giving the keeper a good chance for success.

Not only do modern keepers have access to healthier animals than early boa keepers did, boas are now available in a variety of color and pattern variations. These variations are breathtaking – one can find boas that are almost solid white, black or red, and with many interesting pattern variations that give the snakes an ornate appearance. Many of these animals carry high-price tags that keep them out of range for the average hobbyist, but some are affordable enough that they appear in some pet stores. Even if such snakes are out of your price range, it is nice to know that they exist – a statement that the first generation of boa keepers could not make.

After years of successful maintenance, many keepers begin to consider breeding boa constrictors. When pursued responsibly, with the snakes' well-being in mind, breeding is a wonderful way to enjoy your pets and learn more about the natural world. However, this decision must not be made hastily, as breeding places the animals at increased risk of illness, raises the costs of

Foreword

their maintenance and requires greater efforts on the part of the keeper. When motivated by a passion for the animals, rather than naïve dreams of profiting from the venture, breeding is a worthwhile and important undertaking.

If after learning about these animals and carefully considering your level of commitment, you decide to bring a boa into your life, do so responsibly.

Too many people purchase a boa spontaneously leading to neglected and escaped snakes -- both of which are bad for keepers and the kept. Unfortunately, such outcomes affect conscientious and responsible keepers, who often derive considerable joy and satisfaction from their pet. Bans and restrictions are a common result; in fact, boas are already banned in a number of municipalities.

Do not be part of this problem: Prepare yourself well and learn all you can about these fascinating snakes and the lands from which they hail before acquiring one. Doing so will make you a better keeper, and make your snake better for it.

Chapter 1: Boa Constrictor Basics

1) Description and Anatomy

Although they reach larger sizes than most snakes do, and they represent a very primitive lineage of snakes, boas have anatomy that is largely similar to other snakes. While boas exhibit the same general color pattern throughout their range, the pattern does vary slightly from one subspecies to the next.

Size
While boas are certainly large snakes, as with most other fantastic animals, their size is often exaggerated. Most boa constrictors are about 6 feet long, but they range from about 4 to 12 feet in length.

Size is a sexually dimorphic trait for boas –males average about 6 feet in length, while females often reach 8 feet or more. Additionally, while muscular, male boas remain relatively thin throughout their lives, while adult females attain significant bulk. Whereas a 6-foot-long adult male may only weigh between 10 and 15 pounds, a mature, 8-foot-long female may weigh 50 pounds or more.

Very large boas may be becoming rarer. According to a 2003 field study of Argentine boas (Boa constrictor occidentalis), the maximum recorded length for the subspecies exceeds 12 feet. However, during the five-year study period, the largest animal that the researchers found measured only slightly longer than 9 feet (2.85 meters), (Margarita Chiaraviglio, 2003).

Color Pattern
The color patterns of boas provide the snakes with exceptionally effective camouflage in their native habitats.

Chapter 1: Boa Constrictor Basics

Wild boa constrictors have brown or gray ground colors, the exact hue of which varies with the subspecies, geographical origin and to a lesser extent, individual variation. Many boas begin life with a gray ground color, but most become brown with age. Despite this trend, there is great variation. Many Mexican boas are very dark, as are Argentine boas. Some of the insular forms from Central America, such as Hog Island Boas, are so light that they appear cream colored.

The primary pattern component of boas takes the form of bar-like cross markings, often called saddles. The markings sit along the dorsal surfaces of the snakes, and encroach the lateral surfaces to varying extents. Some saddles are pencil thin while others are quite wide, and resemble the silhouettes of bats or hourglasses. Sometimes they connect with other saddles via thin lines along the edge of the dorsal and lateral surfaces. The number of saddles between the head and the vent are sometimes helpful for distinguishing among subspecies.

Most boas have two light-colored, roughly rectangular spots inside each of the dark saddles. In some individuals, the spots are nearly square, while others bear markings that are very long rectangles.

The lateral surfaces of the body sometimes bear rosettes or other markings. Additionally, scattered black scales often appear on both the dorsal and lateral surfaces. The ventral side is white with numerous black scales. Sometimes the extent of the black scales becomes dense enough to make the ventral surface appear mostly black.

The tail of boa constrictors bears a different pattern and color than the rest of the snake's body. As the pattern moves from the snake's head towards its tail, the dark pattern elements begin to dominate, whereas the light pattern elements (what was formerly the ground color) exhibit reduced size and often, lighter color than along the body. The dark pattern elements often turn red, reddish brown, chestnut, maroon or orange with the change in pattern. This characteristic has led many people to call them "red-

Chapter 1: Boa Constrictor Basics

---

tailed boas." The degree of red coloration varies greatly, although it is characteristic of many subspecies and lineages.

The head is usually the same color as the primary ground color. A single, thin, arrow-shaped line sits along the midline of the head. A dark stripe extends backwards, at a downward angle, from each eye. Assorted black marks dot the sides and lower surfaces of the face.

As with many other snakes, collectors occasionally capture oddly colored or marked specimens from the wild. Those that display minor anomalies may not be at much of a competitive disadvantage, but those that exhibit extremely different color patterns, such as albinos, are unlikely to survive in the wild.

Scalation
The outer covering of a snake's body is comprised of scales. Scales are modified pieces of skin that form in regular rows along the snake's body. Between these scales, the skin is soft and flexible, which allows snakes to stretch to accommodate food items or eggs.

Boa constrictors have smooth, rather than keeled, scales. The scales covering the dorsal and lateral surfaces are diamond shaped, and fit together in a tight matrix. A single row of wide ventral scales covers the bellies of boa constrictors. The subcaudal scales form a single row, although some animals have a few that are split. Boas have fine, round to diamond scales covering most of their heads. They have larger, plate like scales above their lips. These scales bear no indentations like those of many other boa and python species.

Skeletal System
Snakes have elongated bodies, so they have many more vertebrae than most other vertebrates do. Each vertebrae attaches to two rib bones. The degree of flexibility between each vertebra is much greater in constricting snakes, such as boa constrictors, than it is in most non-constricting snakes.

Chapter 1: Boa Constrictor Basics

As demonstrated by their skeletal systems, boas are very primitive snakes. Unlike advanced snakes that hail from more recent lineages, boas have retained the pelvic girdle of their lizard ancestors. However, like all living snakes, boas show no trace of shoulder girdles.

Extending from the pelvic girdle are two rudimentary leg bones. Horny caps cover the end of these bones and penetrate through the body wall, extending outside of the snake's body. These appendages are often referred to as "spurs."

Boas have control over their spurs, but they are not used for locomotion. Males, whose spurs are much longer than those of females, use their spurs to stimulate females during courting. Very large males often have considerably massive spurs, which can scratch a keeper if handled carelessly.

The difference in size between the spurs of males and females is consistent enough that spur length is often considered an accurate method for sexing mature boas.

Internal Organs
Snakes have internal organs that largely mirror those of other vertebrates, with a few exceptions.

The digestive system of snakes is relatively similar to those of other animals, featuring an esophagus that accepts food from the mouth and transports it to the stomach, and long intestines that transport food from the stomach to the anus where the food residue is expelled. Along the way, the liver, gall bladder and pancreas aid the digestive process by producing and storing various digestive enzymes.

Snakes propel blood through their bodies via a heart and circulatory system. Unlike advanced snakes (such as rat snakes, kingsnakes, vipers and elapids), boa constrictors are very primitive snakes that retain a full-sized – but nonfunctioning – left lung.

Chapter 1: Boa Constrictor Basics

The kidneys of snakes are paired as they are in most other animals, but they have a staggered alignment to allow them to fit inside the body cavity. Snakes produce uric acid as a byproduct of protein synthesis, and expel it through the vent. This uric acid often looks like pieces of chalk, and is not soluble in water.

The nervous system of snakes is largely similar to that of other animals. The brain – which is relatively small and primitive – provides the control over the body by sending impulses through the spinal cord and nerves.

One interesting anatomical feature of boas (and snakes in general) is their flexible windpipe. Known as the glottis, the tube transports air to and from the lungs and resides in the bottom of snakes' mouths. Snakes have the ability to move their glottis in order to breathe while they are swallowing large food items.

Reproductive Organs
Males have paired reproductive structures that they hold inside their tail base. The males evert these organs, termed hemipenes, during mating activities and insert them inside the females' cloacas.

Females have paired reproductive systems, which essentially mirror those of other vertebrates. One key difference is the presence of structures called oviducts. Oviducts hold the male's sperm and accept the ova after they are released from the ovaries during ovulation.

The gender of snakes can be determined by passing a smooth, lubricated steel probe into the cloaca of a snake. When moved posteriorly, the probe will penetrate to a much greater depth in males than in females. This occurs because the inserted probe travels down the inside of one of the hidden hemipenes; when inserted into a female, no such space accepts the probe.

(Novices should not attempt to probe snakes. Most veterinarians, breeders and pet stores will perform the procedure for a nominal fee).

Chapter 1: Boa Constrictor Basics

Head

Unlike the helmet-like skull of mammals, the skull of snakes is a loosely articulated collection of strut- and plate-like bones. This allows them to open their mouth wide enough to eat large prey.

Contrary to popular perception, snakes do not dislocate their jaws when swallowing prey. They simply possess more complex joints than most other animals do. Instead of the mandible connecting directly to the skull (as occurs in humans and most other vertebrates), the mandible of snakes connects to the quadrate bone. The quadrate bone, in turn, connects to the skull. This arrangement allows the quadrate bone to swing down and forward, while the mandible pivots downward and forward as well.

Boas have thermally sensitive areas on some of their facial scales, which allow the snakes to sense heat from their environment. In fact, boas have six different types of receptors that all detect temperatures in slightly different ways. (Düring, 1974) Unlike many pythons and pit vipers, boas do not have any specialized cavities (pits) that contain thermally sensitive organs. Accordingly, boas have inferior heat-detecting abilities when compared to pythons and pit vipers. Whereas pit vipers and pythons are able to detect a mouse (via heat alone) from as much as 11 and 26 inches, respectively; boas only detect this level of heat when the prey is closer than about 6 inches. (Buning, 1983)

Teeth

Boas have numerous sharp, pointed teeth, designed for catching and holding prey. A row of teeth sits along the perimeter of both the upper and lower jaw. Additionally, two parallel rows of teeth attach to the roof of the snakes mouth. Boas continually lose and replace teeth throughout their lives.

Chapter 1: Boa Constrictor Basics

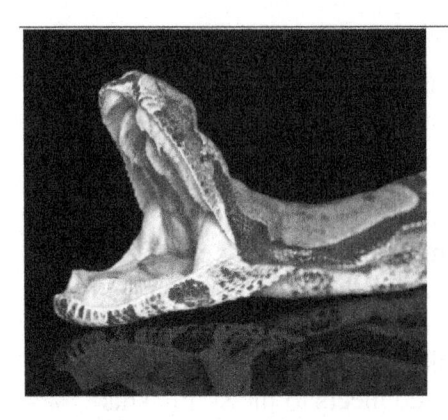

The snake's palatine teeth are visible in this photo.

Eyes

Most boas see movement well, but their acuity may be limited. Boas see well during both the day and the night. While not the most important sensory pathway for boas, (many have survived injuries that left them blind) their sense of sight provides them with a number of advantages.

Snakes lack moveable eyelids, meaning that their eyes are open at all times – even while they sleep. In fact, it can be difficult (or impossible) to tell whether a motionless snake is sleeping or awake. To protect their eye, snakes have a clear scale, called the spectacle. Like all other scales on the snake's body, they shed them periodically.

Boa constrictors have cone cells in their retinas, so they likely have some capacity for perceiving color. Researchers have determined that boa constrictors can see light in the UV portion of the spectrum. (Arnold J. Sillman, 2001) This may help the snakes to find mates and prey. This has already been documented with other species – some hawks search for the ultraviolet signature of rodent urine when hunting. (Withgott, 2000)

Boa constrictors have elliptical pupils that resemble those of a cat. While frequently presumed to be a trait associated with nocturnal activity patterns, recent research indicates that such eyes are more likely an adaptation to ambush – rather than prowling – hunting styles. (F. BRISCHOUX, 2010)

Ears
Snakes lack external ears, but they do have rudimentary middle and inner ears. Part of the reason for this is that the bones which normal reside in the ears of mammals have moved to the jaws of snakes. They now serve as the quadrate bone!

Accordingly, snakes hear very little if at all. Scientists debate the finer points of their abilities, but snakes do not appear to respond to most airborne sounds. However, snakes can feel very low frequency vibrations through the substrate, such as footsteps.

Tongue, Nose and Vomeronasal Organ
The forked tongue of snakes is one of their most famous characteristics. It is exclusively a sensory organ, and it is not used in feeding or sound production.

The tongue extends from the mouth to collect volatile particles from the environment. Then, when the tongue is withdrawn, it transfers these particles to the vomeronasal organ. The vomeronasal organ functions as an additional sense of smell or taste.

The vomeronasal organ (located in the roof of the mouth), has two openings – one for each tip of the snake's tongue. This allows snakes to process directional information picked up by the tongue. Snakes also use their nostrils to detect airborne chemicals in the environment.

In addition to their vomeronasal sense, boas also have a very strong sense of smell.

Chapter 1: Boa Constrictor Basics

Note the bifurcated tongue on this young boa.

Vent
The vent is the place from which snakes defecate and release urates. Additionally, it is the exit point for their reproductive organs and eggs or young. Inside the vent lies a chamber called the cloaca, which holds these products until they are expelled through the vent.

Tail
While they look like heads that seamlessly transition into tails, the tails of snakes are shorter than most people realize they are. The tail starts at the vent (where the spurs are visible) and travels to the end of the body. Boas have strong, prehensile tails that they use to grip branches when climbing.

2) Biology

As with their unique anatomy, snakes exhibit unique biology. In many cases, the physiological differences exhibited by snakes are not as fantastic as they seem, once they are viewed in the correct context.

Shedding
Like other animals, snakes must shed their outer skin layers, as they require replacement. While mammals do so continuously,

Chapter 1: Boa Constrictor Basics

snakes shed their entire external layer of skin cells at periodic intervals.

This process may occur as frequently as once every month when snakes are young and growing quickly, or as rarely as two or three times per year for larger, mature snakes.

Snakes that are injured, ill or parasitized may shed more frequently than usual. Some shedding events, such as the snake's first shed, or the females' post-ovulation shed, mark important milestones.

The shedding process takes approximately 7 to 10 days to complete. Initially, the snake begins producing a layer of fluid between the two outermost layers of skin. This serves as a lubricant that helps the old skin to peel off.

After a day or two, this fluid becomes visible and gives the snakes a cloudy appearance, which, with experience, becomes very easy to spot. It is often most apparent when viewing the snake's ventral surface or eyes. Because a snake's eyes are topped with a clear scale, this fluid makes the eyes look very cloudy and blue. At this time, the snake's vision is impaired, and most spend their time hiding.

A few days later, the snake's eyes clear up, and it looks normal again. A day or two later, the snake will begin the process of shedding.

Snakes begin the process starts by trying to cut the old layer of skin on their lips. They do this by rubbing their faces against stationary surfaces. While many keepers incorporate a rough surface in the cage for fear that the snake will not be able to facilitate his shedding process, in practice, this is rarely a problem. The cage walls are usually more than adequate for the purpose.

After separating the skin on the lips, the old skin starts to peel away. The snake crawls forward, leaving the old skin behind. The new skin usually looks much brighter than normal.

Chapter 1: Boa Constrictor Basics

Metabolism and Digestion

Snakes are ectothermic ("cold-blooded") animals that rely on external sources of heat to drive their metabolisms. This means that, in general, the warmer a snake is, the faster all of the chemical reactions taking place in its body proceed. Snakes that are not warm enough are not able to move, breathe, think or feel stimuli as well as they should.

Boas are able to keep their body temperature relatively constant throughout the day by altering their behavior. They may bask to raise their temperature, and return to a warm retreat, where their body temperature will remain high for an extended period. Additionally, when necessary, boas can keep their body temperature lower than the surrounding area by utilizing cool microhabitats.

Fortunately for boas, the ambient temperatures in their native lands are close to their ideal body temperature. However, while pregnant, digesting food or recovering from illness, boas may bask in the sun. Additionally, they utilize various microhabitats to alter their temperature.

Because large snakes have much less surface area in relation to their volume than small snakes do, they do not heat up or cool off as small snakes do.

Growth Rate and Lifespan

Boa constrictors grow quickly. Young boas are between 12 and 24 inches in length when they are born, and many will exceed 48 inches in length before their second birthday. Males are often mature by their third or fourth year, while most females reach maturity in their fourth year.

While they continue to grow throughout their lives, most boas grow relatively little after reaching maturity. By the time they are 4 or 5 years of age, most boas have essentially reached their final size.

Some breeders have found that if provided with massive amounts of food, boas can grow very quickly. In some cases, boas have

Chapter 1: Boa Constrictor Basics

exceeded 6 feet in length before their first birthday. However, such feeding schedules are not healthy for the animals, and it invariably shortens their lifespan.

Boas are long-lived animals. Those that survive to adulthood probably reach 20 or 30 years of age with regularity. Captive boas, who face no predators, eat consistently and benefit from veterinary care, are quite capable of exceeding this age. A wild-caught animal that lived for 40 years after capture owns the longevity record for the species.

3) Behavior

Hunting and Constriction
Although they may occasionally find food while prowling, boas are largely ambush predators that wait for prey to approach them. They may lie and wait on the ground or in the trees, and during the day or during the night. While all boas can climb, it is more common among smaller individuals – especially juveniles.

When boas spot their prey, they draw their heads back towards their body, in the stereotypical "S-position." When the prey animal comes within range, they strike out and bite it. Almost instantaneously, the boa pulls the animal back towards its body while wrapping coils around the animal.

These strong coils squeeze the prey animal, inhibiting the animal's ability to fill its lungs with oxygen. Most such prey animals likely die from asphyxiation, although some likely die of cardiac arrest instead. Contrary to the old wives' tale, boas do not crush their prey's bones.

Boas have been shown to detect the heart rate of their prey. They appear to use this information to determine when their prey has been incapacitated. At this time, they relax their coils enough to permit them to find the prey's head.

Boas usually consume their prey head first, so that the fur and limbs fold easily against the prey's body, but occasionally they may eat the prey backwards or sideways. This is more common with small prey items than large ones.

Diel Activity
In general, boas are quite adaptable, and often alter their activity patterns to better suit their needs. Boas may be active during the day or the night, even among individuals of the same sex, size class and population (Margarita Chiaraviglio, 2003). However, captive snakes often exhibit greater activity levels after the lights go off.

Although it only investigated a small sample size, a 1969 study by Samuel M. McGinnis and Robert G. Moore found that boas did not bask in the morning to warm up. Rather, they allowed their body temperature to rise naturally, and became active after reaching the desired temperature. (Moore, 1969) However, McGinnis and Moore did report a few instances in which boas basked for short periods of time.

Seasonal Activity
Because they inhabit such a wide latitudinal range, few generalizations can be made about the seasonal habits of boas. Some live on the equator, and experience rather subtle seasonal changes, while others live far enough from the equator that they experience well-defined seasons. No boa lives in areas with winters harsh enough to necessitate hibernation behaviors, although temporary cold weather may cause boas to retreat to underground shelters and remain relatively dormant until suitable temperatures return.

Defensive Strategies and Tactics
Boa constrictors protect themselves from predators in several different ways.

When possible, boas remain hidden to avoid predators; when they must move on the surface, they rely on their cryptic colors and patterns to avoid detection. Additionally, by climbing into the canopy, boas avoid many terrestrial predators.

Chapter 1: Boa Constrictor Basics

If shelter or safety is close by, boas may attempt to crawl away. However, boas are not very fast, and locomotor escape is not a very effective strategy in many cases.

Boas hiss and adopt defensive postures when cornered; if pressed further, they will strike and bite. If necessary, they can attempt to constrict predators. While not a common behavior of boas, they do have the capability to discharge musk and defecate to dissuade predators.

Locomotion
While they may employ several different methods of locomotion, boas primarily crawl via a method called rectilinear motion. However, boas do not hold a monopoly on the method -- rectilinear motion is the most common method of crawling for many large-bodied snakes, including pythons and vipers.

Rectilinear motion occurs when the boas use a section of their ventral and lateral muscles to swing their ventral scales forward, grip the substrate, and then pull the snake forward. The process allows the snakes to crawl forward smoothly, in a straight line.

While they are not as aquatic as their cousins, the Anacondas (*Eunectes* spp.), they swim well and are observed in the water from time to time.

4) Reproductive Behavior and Biology

Boa males track females by using their forked tongues, which pick up volatiles in the environment and then transfer them to the Jacobson's organ. Reproductively active males usually outnumber the reproductively active females in wild boa constrictor populations. Accordingly, an important part of being a male boa is finding suitable mates. In part because of this mating system, males travel more and disperse farther than females do (PAULA C. RIVERA, 2006). Boas often form large aggregations during the breeding season, although the exact nature and purpose of this behavior is not yet understood (Eells, 1968).

Chapter 1: Boa Constrictor Basics

Male boas do not often engage in male-male combat, although it does happen from time to time. This is a common trait in snake species, in which females are the larger sex.

Males often court females for extended periods of time. While doing so, they may ride atop the female's back, while using their spurs to scratch and squeeze her sides near her cloaca. Once the female accepts the male's advances, he will evert one of his hemipenes and insert it into her cloaca. Mating may occur for minutes or hours.

Females store the sperm and ovulate shortly after breeding; at this time, fertilization occurs. The female will hold the young in her abdomen for approximately 125 days following ovulation. At this time, she will give birth to young.

Although boas appear to give live birth to their young, they actually engage in a reproductive method termed ovoviviparity. This means that rather than developing in a uterus and deriving nourishment from a placenta, the young are enclosed in flexible membranes. These membranes are essentially non-calcified eggs. Rather than depositing calcified eggs at an early point in the gestation process, female boas retain these non-calcified eggs in their abdomens until their development is complete. The membranes break during or shortly after the young are born. Researchers have yet to document incidences of boas providing parental care for their young – it is likely that they

While it is an extremely rare phenomenon, researchers have documented boas producing young via parthenogenesis (Warren Booth, 2010).

Chapter 2: Classification and Taxonomy

Originally, boas were considered a single entity – the species *Boa constrictor*. However, as researchers studied boas in greater detail, regional differences became apparent. Subsequently, researchers began describing various boa subspecies.

Nevertheless, the classification of boas is in a perpetual state of flux. It appears that this wide-ranging complex is full of subtlety and regional variation. All boa constrictors are currently considered members of the same species, but some authorities recognize as many as 11 subspecies.

Currently researchers are using genetic tools to investigate the interrelationships of the various subspecies. While such technology has been very illuminating, it has raised nearly as many questions as it has answers.

For example, some studies have suggested that Coastal Peruvian boas are the same biological entity as long-tailed boas are. However, the two types clearly have visual differences.

Other examples of conflicting studies concern Mexican and Central American boas. While some studies have found differences between the two forms, others suggest that they are the same biological entity.

For the average hobbyist, these taxonomic arguments mean relatively little. The vast majority of boa constrictors in the pet trade are common boas (*Boa constrictor imperator*) from Central America or Columbia. However, Boa constrictors (*Boa constrictor constrictor*) from Columbia, Suriname and Guyana are common among boa enthusiasts, as are Argentine boas (*Boa constrictor occidentalis*).

Some boa fans also keep Peruvian long-tailed boas (*Boa constrictor longicauda*), Coastal Peruvian boas (*Boa constrictor*

Chapter 2: Classification and Taxonomy

ortonii) and Mexican boas (*Boa constrictor mexicana*), although some are quite expensive.

Some forms, notably the insular species, are very rare in captivity. The Taboga Island boa may be extinct in the wild.

While there are as many proposed classification schemes as there are researchers, most current boa taxonomies list the group as follows:

Subspecies	Common Name	Range
amarali	Short-tailed Boa	Bolivia, Brazil, Paraguay
constrictor	Boa Constrictor	Columbia south to Bolivia
imperator	Central American Boa	Mexico south to Panama
longicauda	Long-tailed Boa	Northern Peru
mexicana	Mexican Boa*	Northern Mexico
nebulosa	Clouded Boa	Dominica
occidentalis	Argentine Boa	Argentina, Southern Bolivia
orophias	St. Lucian Boa	St. Lucia
ortonii	Coastal Peruvian Boa	Northern Peru
sabogae	Pearl Island Boa	Taboga Island
melanogaster	Black-bellied Boa*	Peru

* = Not universally recognized

Chapter 3: The Boa Constrictor's World

1) Range

Boa constrictors are restricted to the new world. They range from Mexico south through Central America, and into South America, as far as Argentina. Additionally, boa constrictors have colonized many islands, including several in the Greater and Lesser Antilles.

In addition to their historic range, boas have been introduced to several other areas, including south Florida and the island of Cozumel. In such places, the native fauna, which have not adapted to the presence of large, predatory snakes, are experiencing drastic population declines as a result. With unexploited food sources and few predators of their own, boas attain very high densities in such places. During a 1999 study of the island, researchers found 1.8 boas per every 100 kilometers of forest surveyed (Miguel Angel Martínez-Morales, 1999).

Boa constrictors were first documented on the island of Aruba in 1999; by 2003, 273 animals (representing all size classes) were found, including females of over 8 feet in length (John S. Quick, 2005).

Boa constrictors exhibit considerable variation across this range, primarily relating to body size and color pattern. In general, boas display the darkest colors at the northern and southern ends of the species range. The largest specimens likely occur in the rainforest of South America. Many insular forms, subspecies and species exhibit the most divergence from the norm, likely due to their limited gene pools. Many of these isolated forms fail to reach

Chapter 3: The Boa Constrictor's World

large sizes. Some, such as the populations hailing from Hog Island display very light colors.

2) Habitat

Boa constrictors are primarily associated with forests, although they are adaptable animals that also inhabit grasslands, caves, wetlands and riparian areas. They appear to prefer forest edges and clearings, likely because of the increased availability of sunlight (for thermoregulation) and increased prey (which is often higher near forest edges).

Boas are primarily found near sea level, but they have been found at elevations of up to 3,300 feet (1,000 meters).

In the central part of the species' range, most of the forests are best described as wet-broadleaf forests (rainforests). At the northern and southern end of the specie's range, xeric (dry) forests become more common.

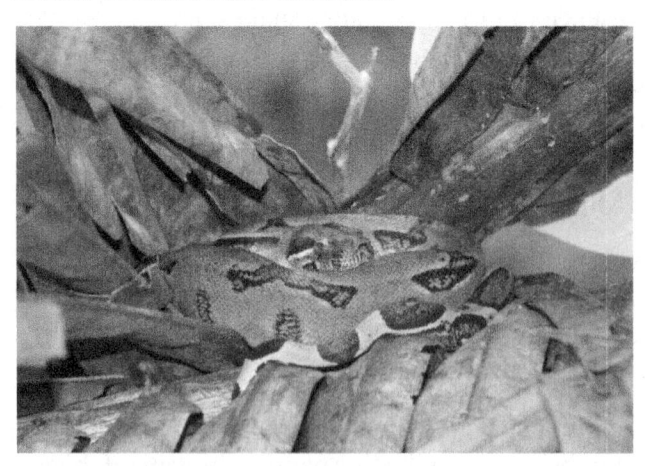

A young boa camouflaging in its natural habitat

A 2007 study of an introduced population of boa constrictors on the island of Cozumel, Mexico, found that the boas utilized all of the major habitats on the island. However, the lowest densities were found around human-disturbed areas, regardless of the surrounding habitat quality. Unfortunately, the researchers also found the most dead snakes in these human-dominated areas (Irene Romero-Nájera, 2007).

Nevertheless, in some areas boa constrictors are often seen near developed and agricultural areas.

3) Natural Diet

Boas are generalist predators that consume a wide variety of prey species. As juveniles, they primarily feed on lizards, small rodents, small birds and, possibly, amphibians. Adults primarily eat mammalian prey, but birds and reptiles form significant portions of the diet of some populations and individuals.

Perhaps the most important prey species for boas are rodents, such as rats, mice and squirrels. Additionally, boas are known to predate on, and live in the burrows of, opossums. This provides an important service for humans living alongside the boas, as opossums often carry and transmit diseases, such as leishmaniasis. By predating on the opossums, and keeping their populations in check, boas help protect the health of humans.

Over the course of 48 hours, scientists working in Brazil documented three individual boa constrictors ambushing small songbirds while perched in a single trumpet tree (*Cecropia* sp.). Two of the snakes successfully captured and ate a bird, while one attempt was unsuccessful and the bird escaped. (Gilson da Rocha-Santos, 2014)

Some of the boa's prey species include intelligent animals, such as coatis and primates. Coatis have been documented defending members of their group against boa constrictors. (Janzen, 1970) Many primates have stereotyped predator calls, and some have specific calls for snakes.

4) Natural Predators

There are very few recorded observations of predators attacking or consuming boa constrictors. However, they undoubtedly serve as prey for other sympatric predators – particularly the juveniles.

Chapter 3: The Boa Constrictor's World

Important predators of juveniles likely include:

- Medium to large birds of prey
- Coatis and opossums
- Ophiophagus snakes, such as the mussurana (*Clelia* spp.)
- Large predatory fish
- Cats
- Canines

Adult boa constrictors face fewer predators. The most important predators of adults are:

- Jaguars
- Crocodilians
- Canines
- Humans

5) Other Sources of Mortality

In addition to predators, boas face several other threats in their natural habitats:

- Road mortality
- Habitat destruction
- Collection for the pet trade
- Storms / floods / fire
- Illness
- Parasites

Chapter 4: The Boa Constrictor as a Pet

While boas can make great pets, there are a number of things to consider before you acquire one of your own. Boa constrictors are living, breathing creatures that deserve the highest quality of life possible.

Warning: Boa constrictors can be dangerous animals when not treated with respect. They are not suitable pets for children.

1) Understanding the Commitment

You will be responsible for your snake's well-being for the rest of its life. This is important to understand, as boa constrictors may live to be 30 years of age or more. One wild caught boa constrictor survived for over 40 years in captivity. Can you be sure that you will still want to care for your pet in 30 or 40 years?

It is not your snake's fault if your interests change. Neglecting your snake is wrong, and in some locations, a criminal offense. You must never neglect your pet, even once the novelty has worn off, and it is no longer fun to clean the cage.

Once you purchase a boa constrictor, its well-being becomes your responsibility until it passes away at the end of a long life, or you have found someone who will agree to take over the care of the animal for you. Understand that it may be very difficult to find someone who will adopt it for you.

Never release a pet snake into the wild.

Snakes introduced to places outside their native range can cause a variety of harmful effects on the ecosystem. Even if the snake is native to the region, it is possible that it has been infected with pathogens. If released into the wild, these pathogens may run rampant through the local population, causing horrific die offs.

Chapter 4: The Boa Constrictor as a Pet

Boa constrictors have been introduced into many places outside of their natural range at the hands of unscrupulous hobbyists. While often overshadowed by the problems caused by Burmese pythons (*Python bivittatus*), boas also cause harm to native ecosystems. This leads to restrictive legislation and casts a bad light on the entire snake-keeping hobby.

2) The Costs of Captivity

Keeping a snake is much less expensive than many other pets; however, novices frequently fail to consider the total costs of purchasing the snake, its habitat, food and other supplies. In addition to the up-front costs, there are on-going costs as well.

Startup costs
One surprising fact for most new keepers is that the enclosure and equipment will often cost about twice what the animal does (this is not always the case with high-priced snakes). In some cases, the total habitat may cost three times the purchase price of the snake or more.

Prices fluctuate from one market to the next, but in general, the least you will spend on the snake is about $50 (£30), while the least you will spend on the *initial* habitat (and assorted equipment) will be $100 (£58).

Conversely, if you select an expensive snake and an elaborate habitat, you could easily spend more than $500 (£292).

Breeders and those with large collections often implement systems that reduce the per-snake housing costs, sometimes getting the costs down to one quarter of that price. However, for the hobbyist with a pet snake or two, such options are not helpful or appropriate.

Examine the charts on the following pages to get an idea of three different pricing scenarios. While the specific prices listed will vary based on numerous variables, the charts are instructive for first-time buyers.

Chapter 4: The Boa Constrictor as a Pet

The first details a keeper who is trying to spend as little as possible, while the second provides a middle-of-the-road example. The third example is of a more extravagant shopper, who wants an expensive snake, and top-notch equipment.

These charts do not cover all of the costs necessary at startup, such as the initial veterinary visit, shipping charges for the snake or any of the equipment (which can easily exceed $100) or the initial food purchase. These charts also fail to allocate anything decorative items, and they assume the use of newspaper as a substrate, which is essentially free.

Inexpensive Option

Common boa (*B. c. imperator*)	$50 (£29)
Plastic Storage Box	$10 (£6)
Screen and Hardware for Lid	$10 (£6)
Heat Lamp Fixture and Bulbs	$20 (£11)
Digital Indoor-Outdoor Thermometer	$15 (£9)
Infrared Thermometer	$35 (£20)
Water Dish	$5 (£3)
Forceps, spray bottles, miscellaneous supplies	$20 (£11)
Total	**$165 (£96)**

Moderate Option

Albino common boa (*B. c. imperator*)	$200 (£120)
20-Gallon Aquarium	$40 (£24)
Screen Lid	$10 (£6)
Heat Lamp Fixture and Bulbs	$20 (£11)
Digital Indoor-Outdoor Thermometer	$15 (£6)
Infrared Thermometer	$35 (£20)
Water Dish	$5 (£3)
Forceps, spray bottles, miscellaneous supplies	$20 (£11)
Total	**$345 (£201)**

Premium Option

Peruvian boa constrictor (*B. c. ortonii*)	$350 (£209)

Chapter 4: The Boa Constrictor as a Pet

Commercial Plastic Cage	$150 (£87)
Radiant Heat Panel	$75 (£44)
Thermostat	$50 (£29)
Digital Indoor-Outdoor Thermometer	$15 (£6)
Infrared Thermometer	$35 (£20)
Water Dish	$5 (£3)
Forceps, spray bottles, miscellaneous supplies	$20 (£11)
Total	**$700 (£409)**

Ongoing Costs

Once you have your snake and his habitat, you must still be able to afford regular care and maintenance. While snakes are low-cost pets, this must be viewed in context.

Compared to a 100-pound Labrador retriever, a snake is relatively inexpensive. However, when compared to a goldfish, tarantula or hermit crab, snakes are fantastically expensive.

Here is an example of the ongoing costs a typical snake keeper must endure. Remember: Emergencies can happen. You must have some way to weather these storms, and afford a sudden $500 (£292) veterinary bill, or the cost to replace a cage when it breaks unexpectedly.

The three primary ongoing costs for snake are:

- **Veterinary Costs**

While experienced keepers may be able to avoid going to the vet for regular observations, novices should visit their veterinarian at least once every six months. Depending on your vet's advice, you may only need to pay for an office visit. However, if your vet sees signs of illness, you may find yourself paying for cultures, medications or procedures. Wise keepers budget at least $200 to $300 (£117 to £175) for veterinary costs each year.

- **Food Costs**

Young boas eat an average of one food item per week, but they may refuse the odd meal because they are shedding or simply do not want to eat. As they mature, they can be fed less frequently – once every second or third week. However, some keepers continue to offer them small, weekly meals. There are pros and cons for each approach, but as long as you provide the proper total amount of food, either strategy will work.

Most young boas will consume about 40 meals per year. The food costs depend on the size of the food items offered, and the route by which you acquire the food items.

For example, a small adult mouse is sufficiently large to satiate most newborn boas, while adult females require very large rats, or other prey, such as chickens or rabbits. This difference in prey size represents at least a ten-fold difference in per-meal food costs.

The other primary factor influencing food costs is the source you use. Retail rodents are about three times the price of those purchased in bulk. However, to purchase bulk rodents, you must have a dedicated freezer in which to keep them. For those with one or two pet snakes, this is hardly cost effective.

Because of these factors, the cost to feed your boa can vary by an order of magnitude depending on its size and your source for prey items. For example, a year's worth of food for a juvenile boa (about 50 mice) purchased in bulk costs about $25 (£15). However, an adult female likely requires at least 12 or more rabbits per year; if purchased in bulk, the total cost would likely be less than $100 (£60), but if you must purchase the rabbits at a retail establishment, the costs are likely to exceed $300 (£180).

- **Maintenance Costs**

It is important to plan for routine and unexpected maintenance costs. Commonly used items, such as paper towels, disinfectant and aspen shavings are rather easy to calculate.

However, it is not easy to know how many burned out light bulbs, cracked water dishes or faulty thermostats you will have to replace in a given year.

Keepers who keep small boas in simple enclosures will likely find that $50 (£29) covers their yearly maintenance costs. By contrast, those keeping large boas in elaborate habitats are sure to spend $200 (£117) or more each year.

Always try to purchase frequently used supplies, such as light bulbs, paper towels and disinfectants in bulk to maximize your savings. It is often beneficial to consult with local reptile-keeping clubs, who often use their members combined needs to make purchases in bulk.

3) Myths and Misunderstandings

Snakes are the subject of countless myths and misunderstandings. It is important to rectify any flawed perceptions before welcoming a snake into your life.

Myth: Snakes grow in proportion to the size of their cage and then stop.

Fact: Snakes do no such thing. Healthy snakes grow throughout their lives, although the rate of growth slows with age. Placing them in a small cage in an attempt to stunt their growth is an unthinkably cruel practice, which is more likely to sicken or kill the snake than stunt its growth.

Myth: Snakes can sense fear.

Fact: Snakes are not magical creatures. They are constrained by physics and biology just as humans, dogs and squid are. That said, it is possible for some animals to read human body language as well as, or better than, other humans. Some long-time keepers have noticed differences in the behavior of some snakes when people of varying comfort levels handle them. This difference in behavior may be confused with the snake "sensing fear."

Chapter 4: The Boa Constrictor as a Pet

Myth: Snakes must eat live food.

Fact: While snakes primarily hunt live prey in the wild, some species consume carrion when the opportunity presents itself. In captivity, most snakes learn to accept dead prey. Whenever possible, hobbyists should feed dead prey to their snakes to minimize the suffering of the prey animal and reduce the chances that the snake will become injured.

Myth: Snakes have no emotions and do not suffer.

Fact: While snakes have very primitive brains, and do not have emotions comparable to those of higher mammals, they can absolutely suffer. Always treat snakes with the same compassion you would offer a dog, cat or horse.

Myth: Snakes prefer elaborately decorated cages that resemble their natural habitat.

Fact: While snakes do thrive better in complex habitats that offer a variety of hiding and thermoregulatory options, they do not appreciate your aesthetic efforts.

Unlike humans, who experience the world through their eyes, snakes experience the world largely as they perceive it through their vomeronasal system. Your snake is not impressed with the rainforest wallpaper decorating the walls of his cage.

Additionally, while snakes require hiding spaces, they do not seem to mind whether this hiding space is in the form of a rock, a rotten log or a paper plate. As long as the hiding spot is safe and snug, they will utilize it.

Myth: Boa constrictors automatically constrict any animal with which they come into contact.

Fact: Boa constrictors are very strong constrictors, but they do not engage in constricting behavior unless they are trying to subdue prey or, rarely, when defending themselves from predators. However, when held, boa constrictors often hang on tightly, but

Chapter 4: The Boa Constrictor as a Pet

this is of little concern. Nevertheless, it is a bad idea to allow any constricting snake to wrap around your neck.

Myth: Boa constrictors are tame snakes that never bite.

Fact: While many boa constrictors are calm and docile animals, they are still wild animals that may behave in unpredictable ways. You should always avoid placing the snake near your (or anyone else's) face in case they do bite. Bites from smaller boa constrictors do not normally cause serious wounds, but bites from larger animals (of about 6 feet or more in length) may cause serious injuries. No matter how long you have owned a snake, always practice safe handling.

4) Acquisition and Selection

The various boa species and subspecies come in so many different colors, patterns, sizes and personalities that it is difficult for a beginner to know where to start.

There are three primary considerations to make:

The Form (Species, Subspecies of Geographic Variant)
Research the various boa species and subspecies to determine which one's characteristics appeal to you. The personality, feeding habits, natural history and size are all important aspects to consider, as is the range of the species.

Ideally, beginners should usually begin with common boas (*Boa constrictor imperator*), as they are very hardy, and often docile, animals. However, with a little extra effort, you can likely succeed with one of the other forms, if, for example, you have your heart set on a Brazilian red-tail boa (*Boa constrictor constrictor*) or an Argentine boa (*Boa constrictor occidentalis*).

The Gender
While the care of both genders is essentially identical (except for breeding maintenance), there are a few reasons for novice keepers to select males over females.

Chapter 4: The Boa Constrictor as a Pet

The single greatest reason is that female boas attain nearly double the size of males. This makes it necessary to feed females more and provide them with larger cages. Because they are much larger, females also represent a larger risk of injuries resulting from bites than males do. Additionally, males are often available at lower prices than females are, because breeders desire for females, which inflates their price.

The Age
Whenever possible, new keepers should elect to purchase animals that are at least a few months old. Newborns often require some skill to get started feeding, so opt for a several-month-old animal that is already well established.

Adult animals are often more intimidating to new keepers than smaller animals are. Choosing a smaller, less intimidating animal is helpful for many new keepers. There is also uncertainty regarding an adult's health and reproductive history, unless the snake comes from a very reliable source.

New keepers certainly can care for adults, but young animals are the better choice.

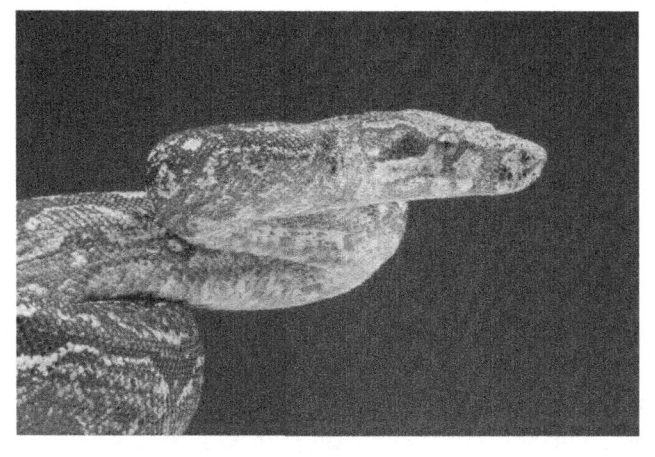

An Argentine boa (Boa constrictor occidentalis).

Chapter 4: The Boa Constrictor as a Pet

The Personality
Advanced hobbyists and breeders may consider a snake's personality to be a low priority in comparison to its species, gender, age and other factors. However, for the pet snake owner, personality is a very important factor.

While snakes are not individuals in the sense that humans or dogs are, they do vary in personality. Some are inherently docile, while a small percentage of any litter may be downright hostile. Some are very shy, while others are more prone to prowling and exploring their cages. While these differences are often very subtle, they do exist, and it behooves the keeper to select a snake with a good personality.

Only rarely will you be able to select a snake from within a collection of his siblings, but if you are, look for the one that is the least defensive. Ironically, these defensive snakes – which are the most likely to bite – are often the quickest ones to initiate feeding. But, as handling and interaction are often important to new keepers, it is best to begin with a tame snake.

5) Acquiring Your Boa

If, after careful, deliberate, consideration, you choose to purchase a boa constrictor, you have a number of places, from which you can obtain one.

Pet Stores
Pet stores are a common place that many people turn to when they decide to purchase a snake. The benefits of shopping at a pet store are that they will likely have all of the equipment you may need, including cages, heating devices and food items. You will usually be able to inspect the snake up close and handle it before purchase. In some cases, you may be able to choose from more than one specimen. Further, many pet stores provide health guarantees for a short period. However, pet stores are retail establishments, and as such, you will pay more than you will from a breeder. Pet stores do not often know the pedigree of the

Chapter 4: The Boa Constrictor as a Pet

animals they sell, nor are they likely to have date of birth, or other pertinent information on the snake.

Reptile Expos

Reptile expos are often excellent places to acquire new animals. Reptile expos often feature resellers, breeders and retailers in the same room, all selling various types of snakes and other reptiles. Often, the prices at such events are quite reasonable and you are often able to select from many different snakes. However, if you have a problem, it may be difficult to find the seller after the event is over.

Breeders

Breeders are the best place for most novices to shop. Breeders generally offer unparalleled information and support after the sale. Additionally, breeders often know the species well, and are better able to help you learn the husbandry techniques for the animal. The disadvantage of buying from a breeder is that you must often make such purchases from a distance, either by phone or via the Internet. Breeders often have the widest selection of snakes, and are often the only place to find rare species or color mutations.

Classified Advertisements

Newspaper and website classified advertisements sometimes include listings for boa constrictors. While individuals, rather than businesses generally post these, they are a viable option to monitor. Often these sales include a snake and all of the associated equipment, which is convenient for new keepers. However, be careful to avoid purchasing someone else's "problem" (i.e. a snake that does not eat or is not docile).

6) Quarantine

Because new animals may have illnesses or parasites that could infect the rest of your collection, it is wise to quarantine any new acquisitions. This means that you should keep the new animal as separated from the rest of your pets as much as possible, until you have ensured that the new animal is healthy.

Chapter 4: The Boa Constrictor as a Pet

During the quarantine period, you should keep the new snake in a simplified habitat, with a paper substrate, water bowl and hiding spot. Keep the temperature and humidity levels at ideal levels, as per normal.

While the animal is being quarantined, visit the veterinarian to ensure the snake does not have any lurking illnesses. Your veterinarian can also double check to ensure no external parasites are present. If possible, a fecal examination should be conducted, to ensure the animal does not have any internal parasites.

Always tend to quarantined animals last, to reduce the chances of transmitting pathogens to your healthy animals. Do not wash water bowls or cage furniture with those belonging to your healthy animals. Whenever possible, use completely separate tools for quarantined animals and those that have been in your collection for some time.

Always be sure to wash your hands thoroughly after handling quarantined snakes, their cages or their tools. Particularly careful keepers wear a smock or alternative clothing when handling quarantined animals.

Quarantine new acquisitions for a minimum of 30 days; 60 or 90 days is even better. Many zoos and professional breeders maintain 180- or 360-day-long quarantine periods.

Most professional breeders and advanced hobbyists maintain their snakes in a state of perpetual quarantine. While they may be kept in the same room with other boas, their dishes, hide boxes and cages are not shared.

Chapter 5: Providing the Captive Habitat

Chapter 5: Providing the Captive Habitat

1) Enclosure

Providing your boa constrictor with appropriate housing is an essential aspect of captive care. In essence, the habitat you provide to your snake becomes his "world."

In "the old days," those inclined to keep snakes had few choices with regard to caging. The two primary options were to build a custom cage from scratch or construct a lid to use with a fish aquarium.

By contrast, modern hobbyists have a variety of options from which to choose. In addition to building custom cages or adapting aquaria, dozens of different cage styles are available – each with different pros and cons.

Dimensions
Throughout their lives, snakes need a cage large enough to lay comfortably, access a range of temperatures and get enough room for exercise.

A good rule of thumb is to ensure that the snake is no longer than ½ of the cage's perimeter.

For example, a 55-gallon aquarium is about 48 inches long by 12 inches deep. This means that the perimeter of the aquarium is about 120 inches long, or 10 feet. Half of this is 60 inches / 5 feet, meaning that such an aquarium could comfortably house a 5-foot-long boa. By way of another example, consider that a 10-gallon aquarium is about 20 inches long, by 11 inches wide. With a perimeter of 62 inches, the cage is suitable for a young boa that is only about 30 inches long.

Chapter 5: Providing the Captive Habitat

Remember, this rule is a guideline for the *minimum* amount of space your snake requires. Always strive to offer the largest cage that you reasonably can. While many keepers suggest that large cages are intimidating to snakes, the truth is more subtle. Contrary to the popular notion, large cages –in and of themselves – do not cause snakes to experience stress.

Snakes live in habitats that exceed even the largest cages by several orders of magnitude. What snakes do not do, however, is spend much time exposed. Even when boas adopt ambush postures while waiting for prey, they often remain partially concealed. Large, barren cages that do not feature complex cage props and numerous hiding places may very well stress snakes. However, large, complex habitats afford more space for exercising and exploring in addition to allowing for the establishment of a superb thermal gradient.

In addition to total space, the layout of the cage is also important – rectangular cages are strongly preferable for a variety of reasons:

- They allow the keeper to establish more drastic heat gradients.
- Cages with one long direction allow your snake to stretch out better than square cage do.
- Front opening cages are easier to maintain when the cages are rectangular, as you do not have to reach as far back into the cage to reach the back wall.

Aquariums

Aquariums are popular choices for snake cages, largely because of their ubiquity. Virtually any pet store that carries snakes also stocks aquariums.

Aquariums can make suitable snake cages, but they have a number of drawbacks. Aquariums are designed with fish in mind, not snakes; accordingly, most of the interior space is arranged in the vertical plane. Additionally, glass cages are hard to clean, and they are easy to break while you are carrying them around.

Chapter 5: Providing the Captive Habitat

While aquaria may work for small boas, boas longer than about 5 feet require very large aquaria, which are difficult to find, expensive to purchase and extremely heavy. While many hobbyists initially purchase a 10-gallon aquarium, it is more cost effective to begin with a 20-gallon or larger aquarium, which will last a lot longer – A 10-gallon aquarium is suitable for boas up to about 30 inches, while a 20-gallon aquarium is suitable for boas up to about 43 inches.

Aquariums are only enclosed on five sides, so keepers have to purchase or build a suitable lid for the enclosure. After-market screen tops are available, but be sure to purchase one that is suitably secure.

Commercial Cages
Commercially produced cages have a number of benefits over other enclosures. Commercial cages usually feature doors on the front of the cage, allowing them to provide better access than top-opening cages do. Additionally, bypass glass doors or framed, hinged doors are generally more secure than after-market screened lids (as are used on aquariums) are.

Additionally, plastic cages are usually produced in dimensions that make more sense for snakes, and often have features that aid in heating and lighting the cage.

Commercial cages can be made out of wood, metal, glass or other substances, but the majority are made from PVC or ABS plastic.

Commercially cages are available in two primary varieties: those that are molded from one piece of plastic and those that are assembled from several different sheets. Assembled cages are less expensive and easier to construct, but molded cages have few (if any) seems or cracks in which bacteria and other pathogens can hide.

Some cage manufacturers produce cages in multiple colors. White is probably the best color for novices, as it is easy to see dirt, mites and other small problems. A single mite crawling on a white cage surface is very visible, even from a distance.

Chapter 5: Providing the Captive Habitat

Black cages do not show dirt as well. This can be helpful for more experienced keepers who have developed proper hygiene techniques over time. Additionally, colorful boa constrictors are often beautiful when viewed against black cage walls.

While boas have cone cells in their retinas, and can presumably see color, it is unlikely that cage color is a significant factor in their quality of life. If you worry about the selection of color, it is probably best to choose a dark or earth-toned color.

Plastic Storage Containers
Plastic storage containers, such as those used for shoes, sweaters or food, make suitable cages for small boas if they are customized to make them secure. The lids for plastic storage boxes are almost never secure enough to be used for snakes without the addition of supplemental security measures.

Hobbyists and breeders overcome this by incorporating Velcro straps, hardware latches or other strategies into plastic storage container cages. While these can be secure, you must be sure they are 100 percent escape-proof before placing a boa in such cages.

The safest way to use plastic storage containers is with the use of a wooden or plastic rack. Such systems are often designed to use containers without lids. In these "lidless" systems, the shelves of the rack form the top to the cage sitting below them. The gap between the top of the sides of the storage containers and the bottom of the shelves is usually very tight – approximately one-eighth inch (2 millimeters) or less.

When plastic containers are used, you must drill or melt numerous holes for air exchange. If you are using a lid, it is acceptable to place the holes in the lid; however, if you are using a lidless system, you will have to make the holes in the sides of the boxes.

Drill or melt all of the holes from the inside of the box, towards the outside of the box. This will help reduce the chances of leaving sharp edges inside the cage, which could cut the snake.

Chapter 5: Providing the Captive Habitat

Homemade Cages
For keepers with access to tools and the desire and skill to use them, it is possible to construct homemade cages. However, this is not recommended for novice keepers, who do not yet have experience with keeping snakes.

A number of materials are suitable for cage construction, and each has different pros and cons. Wood is commonly used, but must be adequately sealed to avoid rotting, warping or absorbing offensive odors.

Plastic sheeting is a very good material, but few have the necessary skills, knowledge and tools necessary for cage construction. Additionally, some plastics may have extended off-gassing times.

Glass can be used, whether glued to itself or when used with a frame. Custom-built glass cages can be better than aquariums, as you can design them in dimensions that are appropriate for snakes. Additionally, they can be constructed in such a way that the door is on the front of the cage, rather than the top.

Screen Cages
Screen cages make excellent habitats for some lizards and frogs, but they are poorly suited for boa constrictors. Screened cages do not retain heat well, and they are hard to keep suitably humid. Additionally, they are difficult to clean. Screen cages are prone to developing week spots that can give the inhabitant enough of a hole to push through and escape.

2) Temperature

Providing the proper thermal environment is one of the most important aspects of snake husbandry. As ectothermic ("cold blooded") animals, snakes rely on the local temperatures to regulate the rate at which their metabolism operates. Providing a proper thermal environment can mean the difference between keeping your pet healthy and spending your time at the veterinarian's office, battling infections and illness.

Chapter 5: Providing the Captive Habitat

While there is variation from one form to the next, boas prefer to keep their body between about 80 and 86 degrees Fahrenheit (26 to 30 degrees Celsius). However, they should not be kept at such temperatures constantly – snakes benefit from cooler nights and the ability to escape warm temperatures through the day. Sometimes they may bask to raise their body temperature over this level.

Most boas live in areas with temperatures near this level, so they do not exhibit the drastic thermoregulatory habits of snakes from less hospitable environments.

3) Thermal Gradients

In the wild, boas move between different microhabitats so that they can maintain ideal body temperature as much as possible.

You want to provide similar opportunities for captive snakes, by creating a thermal gradient.

To establish a thermal gradient, place the heating devices at one end of the habitat. This creates a basking spot, which should have the highest temperatures in the cage. This area should be larger than your snake's coiled body so that he can warm his entire body if he wishes.

Because there is no heat source at the other end of the cage, the temperature will gradually fall as your snake moves away from the heat source.

Ideally, the difference between the coolest spot in the cage and the basking spot will be at least 12 to 14 Fahrenheit (8 to 10 degrees Celsius), and larger if possible. If more than one heat source is required for the habitat, they should be clustered at one end.

The need to establish a thermal gradient is one of the most compelling reasons to use a large cage. In general, the larger the cage, the easier it is to establish a drastic thermal gradient.

Chapter 5: Providing the Captive Habitat

Ideally, boa constrictors should have a basking spot in the low-90s Fahrenheit, while the cool side of the enclosure should be in the high-70s to low-80s.

4) Heat Lamps

Heat lamps are one of the best choices for supplying heat to boas. Heat lamps consist of a reflector dome and an incandescent bulb. The light bulb produces heat (in addition to light) and the metal reflector dome directs the heat to a spot inside the cage.

If you use a cage with a metal screen lid, you can rest the reflector dome directly on the screen; otherwise, you will need to clamp the lamp to something over the cage. Always be sure that the lamp is securely attached and will not be dislodged by vibration, children or pets. Always opt to purchase heavy-duty reflector domes with ceramic bases, rather than economy units with plastic bases.

While you can use specialized light bulbs that are designed for use with reptiles, it is not necessary. Regular, economy, incandescent bulbs work well. Snakes do not require special lighting, and incandescent bulbs – even those produced for use with reptiles – rarely generate much UVA, and never generate UVB.

One of the greatest benefits of using heat lamps to maintain the temperature of your snake's habitat is the inherent (and affordable) flexibility. While heat tapes and other devices are easy to adjust, a rheostat or thermostat is necessary to do so. Such devices are not prohibitively expensive, but they will raise the budget of your snake's habitat.

By contrast, heat lamps offer flexibility in two ways:

Changing the Bulb Wattage

The simplest way to adjust the temperature of your boa's cage is by changing the wattage of the bulb being used. For example, if a 40-watt light bulb is not raising the temperature of the basking

Chapter 5: Providing the Captive Habitat

spot high enough, you may try a 60-watt bulb. Alternatively, if a 100-watt light bulb is elevating the cage temperatures higher than are appropriate, switching the bulb to a 60-watt model may help.

Adjusting the Height of the Heat Lamp

The closer the heat lamp is to the cage, the warmer the cage will be. Use this characteristic to your advantage. For example, if the habitat is too warm, the light can be raised, which should lower the cage temperatures slightly.

However, the higher the heat lamp is raised, the larger the basking spot becomes. Accordingly, it is important to be careful that you do not raise the light too high, which results in reducing the effectiveness of the cage's thermal gradient. In very large cages, this may not compromise the thermal gradient very much, but in a small cage, it may eliminate the "cool side" of the habitat.

In other words, if your heat lamp creates a basking spot that is roughly 1-foot in diameter when it rests directly on the screen, it may produce a slightly cooler, but larger basking spot when raised 6-inches above the level of the screen.

One way to avoid reducing the effectiveness of the gradient is through the use of "spot" bulbs, which produce a relatively narrow beam of light. Such lights may be slightly more expensive than economy bulbs, but because they make heat gradients easier to achieve, they deserve consideration. One problem with using heat lamps is the current trend in which many manufacturers have stopped producing incandescent bulbs. In some municipalities, they may even be illegal to sell. It remains to be seen if incandescent bulbs will remain available to herpetoculturists over the long term or not. Fortunately, many other heating options are available.

5) Ceramic Heat Emitters

Ceramic heat emitters are small inserts that function similarly to light bulbs, except that they do not produce any visible light – they only produce heat.

Chapter 5: Providing the Captive Habitat

Ceramic heat emitters are used in reflector-dome fixtures, just as heat lamps are. The benefits of such devices are numerous:

- They typically last much longer than light bulbs do
- They are suitable for use with thermostats
- They allow for the creation of overhead basking spots, as lights do
- They can be used day or night

However, the devices do have three primary drawbacks:

- They are very hot when in operation
- They are much more expensive than light bulbs
- You cannot tell by looking if they are hot or cool. This can be a safety hazard – touching a ceramic heat emitter while it is hot is likely to cause serious burns.

Ceramic heat emitters are nearly the same price as radiant heat panels are. This causes many to select radiant heat panes over ceramic heat emitters. Radiant heat panels are generally preferable to ceramic heat emitters, as they usually have a light that indicates when they are on, and they do not get as hot on the surface.

6) Radiant Heat Panels

Quality radiant heat panels are the best choice for heating most reptile habitats, including those containing boas. Radiant heat panels are essentially heat pads that stick to the roof of the habitat. They usually feature rugged, plastic or metal casings and internal reflectors to direct the infrared heat back into the cage.

Radiant heat panels have a number of benefits over traditional heat lamps and under tank heat pads:

- They do not contact the animal at all, thus reducing the risk of burns.
- They do not produce visible light, which means they are useful for both diurnal and nocturnal heat production. They can be used in conjunction with fluorescent light

fixtures during the day, and remain on at night once the lights go off.
- They are inherently flexible. Unlike many devices that do not work well with pulse-proportional thermostats, most radiant heat panels work well with on-off and pulse-proportional thermostats.

The only real drawback to radiant heat panels is their cost: radiant heat panels often cost about two to three times the price of light- or heat pad-oriented systems. However, many radiant heat panels outlast light bulbs and heat pads, a fact that offsets their high initial cost over the long term.

7) Heat Pads

Heat pads are an attractive option for many new keepers, but they are not without drawbacks.

- Heat pads have a high risk for causing contact burns.
- If they malfunction, they can damage the cage as well as the surface on which they are placed.
- They are more likely to cause a fire than heat lamps or radiant heat panels are.

However, if installed properly (which includes allowing fresh air to flow over the exposed side of the heat pad) and used in conjunction with a thermostat, they can be reasonably safe. With heat pads, it behooves the keeper to purchase premium products, despite the small increase in price.

8) Heat Tape

Heat tape is somewhat akin to "stripped down" heat pads. In fact, most heat pads are simply pieces of heat tape that have already been connected and sealed inside a plastic envelope.

Heat tape is primarily used to heat large numbers of cages simultaneously. It is generally inappropriate for novices, and

Chapter 5: Providing the Captive Habitat

requires the keeper to make electrical connections. Additionally, a thermostat is always required when using heat tape.

Historically, heat tape was used to keep water pipes from freezing – not to heat reptile cages. While some commercial heat tapes have been designed specifically for reptiles, many have not. Accordingly, it may be illegal, not to mention dangerous, to use such heat tapes to heat reptile cages.

9) Heat Cables

Heat cables are similar to heat tape, in that they heat a long strip of the cage, but they are much more flexible and easy to use. Many heat cables are suitable to use inside the cage, while others are designed for use outside the habitat.

Always be sure to purchase heat cables that are designed to be used in reptile cages. Those sold at hardware stores are not appropriate for use in a cage.

Heat cables must be used in conjunction with a thermostat, or, at the very least, a rheostat.

10) Hot Rocks

In the early days of commercial reptile products, faux rocks, branches and caves with internal heating elements were very popular. However, they have generally fallen out of favor among modern keepers. These rocks and branches were often made with poor craftsmanship and cheap materials, causing them to fail and produce tragic results. Additionally, many keepers used the rocks improperly, leading to injuries, illnesses and death for many unfortunate reptiles.

Heated rocks are not designed to heat an entire cage; they are designed to provide a localized source of heat for the reptile. Nevertheless, many keepers tried to use them as the primary heat source for the cage, resulting in dangerously cool cage temperatures.

Chapter 5: Providing the Captive Habitat

When snakes must rely on small, localized heat sources placed in otherwise chilly cages, they often hug these heat sources for extended periods of time. This can lead to serious thermal burns – whether or not the units function properly. This illustrates the key reason why these devices make adequate supplemental heat sources, but they should not be used as primary heating sources.

Modern hot rocks utilize better features, materials and craftsmanship than the old models did, but they still offer few benefits to the keeper or the kept. Additionally, any heating devices that are designed to be used inside the cage necessitate passing an electric cable through a hole, which is not always easy to accomplish. However, some cages do feature passageways for chords.

11) Thermometers

It is important to monitor the cage temperatures very carefully to ensure your pet stays health. Just as a water test kit is an aquarist's best friend, a quality thermometer is one of the most important husbandry tools for snakes.

Ambient and Surface Temperatures
Two different types of temperature are relevant for pet snakes: ambient temperatures and surface temperatures.

The ambient temperature in your animal's cage is the air temperature. By contrast, surface temperatures are those of the objects in the cage.

For example, the air temperatures may be 90 degrees Fahrenheit (32 degrees Celsius) on a hot summer day. However, the surface of a black rock may be much hotter than this. If you checked the surface temperatures of the rock, they may be in excess of 120 degrees Fahrenheit (48 degrees Celsius).

In general, the ambient temperatures require more frequent monitoring and attention. As long as the surface temperatures of the cage do not exceed about 120 degrees Fahrenheit, your snake

Chapter 5: Providing the Captive Habitat

is not likely to be harmed from incidental contact. However, ambient temperatures of 120 degrees would be fatal very quickly.

Measure the cage's ambient temperatures with a digital thermometer. An indoor-outdoor model will feature a probe that allows you to measure the temperature at both ends of the thermal gradient at once. For example, you may have the thermometer positioned at the cool side of the cage, but the remote probe placed under the basking lamp.

Standard digital thermometers do not measure surface temperatures well. Instead, you should use a non-contact, infrared thermometer. Such devices will allow you to measure surface temperatures accurately and from a short distance away.

12) Thermostats and Rheostats

Some heating devices, such as heat lamps, are designed to operate at full capacity for the entire time that they are turned on. Such devices should not be used with thermostats – instead, care should be taken to calibrate the proper temperature.

Other devices, such as heat pads, heat tape and radiant heat panels are designed to be used with a regulating device to maintain the proper temperature, such as a thermostat or rheostat.

Rheostats
Rheostats are similar to light-dimmer switches, and they allow you to reduce the output of a heating device. In this way, you can dial in the proper temperature for the habitat.

The drawback to rheostats is that they only regulate the amount of power going to the device – they do not monitor the cage temperature or adjust the power flow automatically. In practice, even with the same level of power entering the device, the amount of heat generated by most heat sources will vary over the course of the day.

If you set the rheostat so that it keeps the cage at the right temperature in the morning, it may become too hot by the middle

Chapter 5: Providing the Captive Habitat

of the day. Conversely, setting the proper temperature during the middle of the day may leave the morning temperatures too cool.

Care must be taken to ensure that the rheostat controller is not inadvertently bumped or jostled, causing the temperature to rise or fall outside of healthy parameters.

Thermostats

Thermostats are similar to rheostats, except that they also feature a temperature probe that monitors the temperature in the cage (or under the basking source). This allows the thermostat to adjust the power going to the device as necessary to maintain a predetermined temperature.

For example, if you place the temperature probe under a basking spot powered by a radiant heat panel, the thermostat will keep the temperature relatively constant under the basking site.

There are two different types of thermostats:

- On-Off Thermostats work by cutting the power to the device when the probe's temperature reaches a given temperature. For example, if the thermostat were set to 85 degrees Fahrenheit (29 degrees Celsius), the heating device would turn off whenever the temperature is this high or higher. When the temperature falls below 85, the thermostat will restore power to the unit, and the heater will begin functioning again. This cycle will repeat over and over again, thus maintaining the temperature within a relatively small range.

  Be aware that on-off thermostats have a "lag" factor, meaning that they do not turn off when the temperature reaches a given temperature. They turn off when the temperature is a few degrees *above* that temperature, and then turn back on when the temperate is a little *below* the set point. Because of this, it is important to avoid setting the temperature at the limits of your pet's acceptable

Chapter 5: Providing the Captive Habitat

range. Some premium models have an adjustable amount of threshold for this factor, which is helpful.

- Pulse proportional thermostats work by constantly sending pulses of electricity to the heater. By varying the rate of pulses, the amount of energy reaching the heating devices varies. A small computer inside the thermostat adjusts this rate to match the set-point temperature as measured by the probe. Accordingly, pulse proportional thermostats maintain much more consistent temperatures than on-off thermostats do.

Lights should not be used with thermostats, as the constant flickering may stress your snake. Conversely, heat pads, heat tape, radiant heat panels and ceramic heat emitters should always be used with either a rheostat or, preferably, a thermostat to avoid overheating your snake.

Thermostat Failure
If used for long enough, all thermostats eventually fail – the question is, will your fail today or twenty years from now? While some thermostats fail in the "off" position, a thermostat that fails in the "on" position may overheat your snakes. Unfortunately, tales of entire collections being lost to a faulty thermostat are too common.

Accordingly, it behooves the keeper to acquire high-quality thermostats. Some keepers use two thermostats, connected in series arrangement. By setting the second thermostat (the "backup thermostat") a few degrees higher than the setting used on the "primary thermostat," you safeguard yourself against the failure of either unit.

In such a scenario, the backup thermostat allows the full power coming to it to travel through to the heating device, as the temperature never reaches its higher set-point temperature. However, if the first unit fails in the "on" position, the second thermostat will keep the temperatures from becoming too high. The temperature will rise a few degrees in accordance with the

Chapter 5: Providing the Captive Habitat

higher set-point temperature, but it will not get hot enough to harm your snakes.

If the backup thermostat fails in the "on" position, the first thermostat retains control. If either fails in the "off" position, the temperature will fall until you rectify the situation, but a brief exposure to relatively cool temperatures is unlikely to be fatal.

13) Nighttime Heating

In most circumstances, you should provide your boa with an 8 to 10 degree temperature drop at night. Some keepers achieve success with constant heat, but wild boas are almost invariably exposed to such temperature fluctuations, which may provide some benefits.

To do so, you can simply switch your heating device off at night, and turn it back on in the morning. Alternatively, you can plug the heating devices (and thermostats or rheostats) into a lamp-timer to automate the process. Some thermostats have features that adjust the temperature of the thermostat during the night, lowering it to a specified level.

Others, who must provide some type of nocturnal heat source for their pet, can do so in a number of ways. Virtually any non-light-emitting heat source will function adequately in this capacity. Ceramic heating elements, radiant heat panels and heat pads, cables and tape all work well for supplying nocturnal heat.

Red lights can be used in reflector domes to provide heat as well. In fact, red lights can be used for heating during the day and night, but the cage will not be illuminated very well, unless other lights are incorporated during the day.

14) Incorporating Thermal Mass

One underutilized technique that is helpful for making small changes in the way you heat a cage is by raising the cage's thermal mass. Rocks, large water dishes and ceramic cage decorations are examples of items that may work in such a context. These objects will absorb heat from the heat source, and then re-radiate heat into the habitat.

This changes the thermal characteristics of the habitat greatly. Often, keepers in cool climates benefit from these techniques when trying to warm cages sufficiently. By simply adding a large rock, the cage may eventually warm up a few degrees.

Raising the cage's thermal mass also helps to reduce the cage's rate of cooling in the evening. By placing a thick rock under the basking light, it will absorb heat all day and re-radiate this heat after the lights turn off. Eventually it will reach room temperature, but this may take hours.

Always remember to monitor the cage surface temperatures and ambient temperatures regularly after changing the thermal characteristics of the cage. Pay special attention to the surface temperatures of items placed on or under a heat source.

Experiment with different amounts of thermal mass in the cage. Use items of different sizes, shapes and materials, and see how the cage temperatures change. In general, the more thermal mass in the cage, the more constant the temperature will stay.

15) Room Heat

Some keepers with very large collections elect to heat the entire room, rather than individual cages. While this is an economic and viable solution for advanced keepers, it is not appropriate for novices.

Heating the whole room, instead of an individual cage, makes it very difficult to achieve a good thermal gradient. Experienced keepers may be able to maintain their snakes successfully in this manner, but beginners should always rely on the added safety afforded by a gradient.

Additionally, room heat is rarely cost-effective for a keeper with a pet snake or two. Relying on a single heating source for an entire

Chapter 5: Providing the Captive Habitat

room is also a high-risk proposition; if the heater or thermostat fails in the "on" position, the entire room may overheat.

16) Lights

Boas do not require special or elaborate lighting. Heat lamps provide plenty of illumination for them, while ambient light that enters their cage is sufficient for cages that do not use heat lamps for warmth. However, some keepers prefer to incorporate supplemental lighting to improve the visibility of their snake.

Fluorescent bulbs are the best choice for supplemental lighting. These lights produce light of higher quality than incandescent bulbs do, and they do not produce very much heat.

Full-spectrum lights with a high color-rendering index will make your snake look his best, but even economy bulbs will allow you to see your animal better. Reptile-specific lights are not required for boas, as they do not require exposure to ultraviolet radiation to metabolize their dietary calcium and vitamin D, as many lizards and turtles do.

If heat lamps are used to keep the nighttime temperatures from dropping too low, be sure to use red lights, which are not likely to disrupt the snake's day-night cycle.

Just as you provide a thermal gradient for your snake, ideally, you should provide a photo gradient as well. This will allow the snake to move between dark and light areas, which further replicates his natural lifestyle.

Always measure the cage temperatures after adding or changing the type of light sources used. While fluorescent lights do not produce a lot of heat, they may generate enough to warm small cages to undesirable levels.

17) Security

Because they may reach sizes that allow them to cause harm to people and pets, it is extremely important to consider cage

Chapter 5: Providing the Captive Habitat

security. In most circumstances, if a snake can push its head through a crack, it can usually pull its entire body behind it.

Never use a cage to house a boa constrictor if you are not certain that it is escape proof. Additionally, be sure to inspect all cages regularly to catch problems (such as a fraying bit of screen or a loose door gasket) before they are large enough to permit the snake to escape.

18) Substrate

Substrates are used to give your snake a comfortable surface on which to crawl and to absorb any liquids present. There are a variety of acceptable choices, all of which have benefits and drawbacks. The only common substrate that is never acceptable is cedar shavings, which emits fumes that are toxic to snakes.

Paper Products

The easiest and safest substrates for boas are paper products in sheet form. While regular newspaper is the most common choice, some keepers prefer paper towels, unprinted newspaper, butcher's paper or a commercial version of these products.

Paper substrates are very easy to maintain, but they do not last very long and must be completely replaced when they are soiled. Accordingly, they must be changed regularly -- at least once per week.

Use several layers of paper products to provide sufficient absorbency and a little bit of cushion for the snake.

Aspen

Shredded aspen bark is a popular substrate choice that works very well. Aspen shares most of the concerns that other particulate substrates do (ingestion hazards, increased labor), but it is likely the best of the particulate substrates for boas.

Aspen can be dusty, so look for brands that are advertised as "low dust." Aspen does not resist decay well, which is a drawback when working with species such as boas, which prefer slightly

Chapter 5: Providing the Captive Habitat

---

elevated humidity levels. Nevertheless, some of the largest breeders in the world use aspen substrates successfully with boas.

Aspen can be spot cleaned daily, but like most other particulate substrates, you must replace it completely every month.

Pine
Some keepers worry that the fumes from pinewood may be toxic to snakes. While pine wood shavings can be a cost effective substrate, there are numerous other options that are known to be safe. Note that pine bark mulch should not produce many fumes, and is likely to be safer than the wood. Additionally, pine bark mulch resists decay for longer than mulch made from the wood of the trees, although it eventually does breakdown in damp conditions.

Orchid Bark
The bark of fir trees is often used for orchid propagation, and so it is often called "orchid bark." Orchid bark is very attractive, though not quite as natural looking as pine bark. However, it exceeds pine in most other ways except cost.

Orchid bark absorbs water very well, so keepers who maintain rainforest species often use it.

Because orchid bark is often reddish in color, it is very easy to spot clean. However, monthly replacement can be expensive for those living in the eastern United States and Europe.

Cypress Mulch
Cypress mulch is a popular substrate choice for many tropical species.

One significant drawback to cypress mulch is that some brands (or individual bags among otherwise good brands) produce a stick-like mulch, rather than mulch composed of thicker pieces.

These sharp sticks can injure the keeper and the kept. It usually only takes one cypress mulch splinter jammed under a keeper's fingernail to cause them to switch substrates.

Chapter 5: Providing the Captive Habitat

Pulp Products

Many commercial pulp products have become available over the last decade. Comprised of recycled wood fibers, these products are very absorbent, but pose an ingestion hazard as they may swell once inside a snake's digestive system.

Nevertheless, many keepers prefer pulp products over all other substrates. If these types of substrate are used, care should be taken to ensure the snakes do not swallow any of the substrate.

These products often absorb odors and liquids well, but with proper cage hygiene, snake cages should not emit objectionable odors.

Substrate Comparison Chart

Substrate	Pros	Cons
Newspaper	Safe, free, easiest substrate for keeping the cage clean.	May be unattractive to some. Purchase pre-printed paper if you are uncomfortable with the ink. Cannot be spot-cleaned.
Paper Towels	Safe, highly absorbent.	May be unattractive to some. Cannot be spot-cleaned.
Commercial Paper Product	Safe and easy to maintain.	May be unattractive to some. Can be expensive with long term use. Cannot be spot-cleaned.
Aspen Shavings	Allows snake to burrow, easy to spot-clean.	May be ingested, messy, can be expensive. Rots if it becomes wet.
Pine Bark Mulch	Allows snake to burrow, easy to spot-clean.	May be ingested, messy, can be expensive. Rots if it becomes wet.
Cypress Mulch	Allows snake to	May be ingested,

Chapter 5: Providing the Captive Habitat

	burrow, easy to spot-clean. Many find it attractive. Retains moisture well.	sharp sticks may harm snakes, messy, can be expensive.
Fir (Orchid) Bark	Allows snake to burrow, easy to spot-clean. Many find it attractive. Retains moisture well.	May be ingested, messy, can be expensive.
Pulp Paper Products	Allows snake to burrow, easy to spot-clean.	May be unattractive to some. May be ingested, messy, can be expensive.

19) Cage Furniture

Strictly speaking, it is possible to keep a boa in a cage devoid of anything but a substrate that permits burrowing and a water bowl. However, it is very beneficial to provide complex environments, with numerous hiding opportunities in the cage.

Additionally, many keepers enjoy decorating the cage to resemble the animal's natural habitat. While such measures are not necessary from the snake's point of view, if implemented with care, there is no reason not to decorate your pet's cage, if you are inclined to do so. However, it is recommended that beginners use a simple cage design for their first 6 to 12 months while they learn to provide effective husbandry.

Boas are secretive creatures. If they do not have a reason to expose themselves to predators, they do not. While this is sometimes disappointing to beginning snake keepers, it is necessary to allow your snake to spend much of its time hiding so that it feels secure and stress-free.

Snakes will move about to find water, food, mates or appropriate environmental conditions. Each species (and individual) has a different typical activity level – some of the racers (*Coluber* sp.) and whip snakes (*Masticophis* sp.) may be accustomed to

Chapter 5: Providing the Captive Habitat

traveling many miles each day in search of food, but boa constrictors travel relatively little.

Accordingly, it is imperative to provide your boa constrictor with hiding opportunities.

20) Hide Boxes

"Hide boxes" come in a wide variety of shapes, sizes and styles. Some keepers use modified plastic or cardboard containers, while others use realistic looking logs and wood pieces. Both approaches are acceptable, but all hides must offer a few key things:

- Hides should be safe for the snakes, and feature no sharp edges or toxic chemicals.
- Hides should accommodate the snake, but not much else. They should be only slightly larger than the snake's body when it is laying in a flat coil.
- Hides should have low profiles. Snakes prefer to feel the top of the hide contacting the dorsal surface of their body.
- Hides either must be easy and economical to replace or constructed from materials that are easy to clean.

Plastic Storage Boxes
Just as a plastic storage box can be converted into an acceptable enclosure, small storage boxes can be converted into functional hiding places. Food containers, shoeboxes and butter tubs can serve as the base. If the container has a low profile, it needs only have a door cut into the tub. Alternatively, you can discard the lid, flip the tub upside down and cut an entrance hole in the side.

Plant Saucers
The saucers designed to collect the water that overfills potted plants make excellent hiding locations. All you have to do is flip them upside down and cut a small opening in the side for a door. Clay or plastic saucers can be used, but clay saucers are hard to

cut. If you punch an entrance hole into a clay saucer, you must sand or grind down the edges to prevent hurting your snake.

Plates
Plastic, paper or ceramic plates make good hiding locations for small boas in cages that use particulate substrates. This will allow the snake to burrow up under the plate through the substrate, and hide in a very tight space. Such hiding places also make it very easy to access your snake while he is hiding.

Cardboard Boxes
While you must discard and replace them anytime they become soiled, small cardboard boxes can make suitable hide boxes.

Commercial "Half-Logs"
Many pet stores sell U-shaped pieces of wood that resemble half of a hollow log. While these are sometimes attractive looking items, they are not appropriate hide spots when used as intended. The U-shaped construction means that the snake will not feel the top of the hide when he is laying inside. These hides can be functional if they are partially buried, thus reducing the height of the hide.

Cork Bark
Real bark cut from the Cork Oak (*Quercus suber*), "cork bark" is a wonderful looking decorative item that can be implemented in a variety of ways. Usually cork bark is available in tube shape or in flat sheets. Flat pieces are better for smaller boas, although exceptionally large snakes may be able to use tubular sections adequately. Flat pieces should only be used with particulate, rather than sheet-like substrates so that the snake can get under them easily.

Cork bark may be slightly difficult to clean, as its surface contains numerous indentations and crevices. Use hot water, soap and a sturdy brush to clean the pieces.

Commercially Produced Plastic Hides
Many different manufacturers market simple, plastic, hiding boxes. These are very functional if sized correctly, although some

Chapter 5: Providing the Captive Habitat

brands tend to be too tall. The simple design and plastic construction makes them very easy to clean.

Paper Towel Tubes
Small sections of paper towel tubes make suitable hiding spots for small boas, although the snakes quickly become too large for such hides. They do not last very long, so they require frequent replacement. They often work best if flattened slightly.

Newspaper or Paper Towels
Several sheets of newspaper or paper towels placed on top of the substrate (whether sheet-like or particulate) make suitable hiding spots. Many professional breeders use paper-hiding spaces because it is such a simple and economically feasible solution. Some keepers crumple a few of the sheets to give the stack of paper more height.

Unusual Items
Some keepers like to express their individuality by using unique or unusual items as hiding spots. Some have used handmade ceramic items, while others have used skulls or turtle shells. If the four primary criteria previously discussed are met, there is no reason such items will not make suitable hiding spaces.

21) Humid Hides

In addition to security, snakes also derive another benefit from many of their hiding spaces in the wild. Most hiding places feature higher humidity than the surrounding air.

By spending a lot of time in such places, snakes are able to avoid dehydration in habitats where water is scarce. Additionally, sleeping in these humid retreats aids in the shedding process. You should take steps to provide similar opportunities in captivity.

Humid hides can be made by placing damp sphagnum moss in a plastic container. The moss should not be saturated, but merely damp. You can also use damp paper towels or newspaper to increase the humidity of a hide box.

Chapter 5: Providing the Captive Habitat

Some keepers prefer to keep humid hides in the habitat at all times, while others use them periodically – usually preceding shed cycles. Humid hides should never be the only hides available to the snake. Always use them in addition to dry hides.

22) A Final Word about the Importance of Hides

With relatively few exceptions, snakes will become severely stressed if they are forced to remain in the open at all times. In addition to health problems that may result, it is likely to affect your pet's personality as well. Snakes that are constantly stressed are more likely to exhibit defensive behaviors when they are handled.

In the wild, hiding spaces are rarely difficult for snakes to find. Provide them with the same opportunity in captivity. Because snakes are likely to select security over all other criteria, it is best to place hides at different parts of the thermal gradient. Additionally, it is wise to include humid and dry hides to the greatest extent possible.

23) Climbing Branches

Many wild boas are observed resting or climbing in the trees. Boas are known to use trees as ambush locations, where they hunt both birds and rodents; but they also serve as refuges from terrestrial predators and basking locations.

While captive boas do not require climbing branches, most use them when they are included in the cage design. Accordingly, many keepers like to provide their boas with climbing branches.

The only drawbacks to including branches in the cage design are the minimal costs associated with installing them and the fact that they must be cleaned regularly. On the other hand, they likely improve your pet's quality of life and many boas feed better when perched on a branch than they do when on the ground. Additionally, branches can be placed in such a way that the snake

Chapter 5: Providing the Captive Habitat

perches in a conspicuous place in the cage, which helps to make your pet more visible to observers.

Some boas seem to feel most secure while perched high in the cage, rather than under a hiding spot. This is even more true when foliage or other visual obstructions are placed around the boa's favorite perching spots.

Boas are adaptable snakes that will often take advantage of whatever climbing opportunities are provided to them. However, not all boas are equally willing to climb branches placed in their cage. Maximize the likelihood that your pet will use his branches by implementing these tips:

- Use branches that are wider than the snake's body is. While boas can grip onto much smaller branches, it requires much more effort for them to do so. (Jayne, 2010)
- Place the branches so that they are as close to horizontal as possible.
- Be sure to attach the branches to the cage wall securely, so the branches do not shift or rotate on their axis. Boas do not like to climb on branches that do not feel stable.
- Try to provide several different branches for your snake to spread his weight across. Unlike emerald tree boas (*Corallus caninus*) and green tree pythons (*Morelia viridis*) who like to coil around a single branch, boas prefer to rest at branch junctions.

You can purchase climbing branches from pet and craft stores, or you can collect them yourself. When collecting your own branches, try to use branches that are still attached to trees (always obtain permission first). Such branches are less likely to harbor insects or other invertebrate pests than fallen, dead branches will. Most of the insects that infest wood will cause your snake no harm, but they may scatter frass (insect droppings mixed with wood shavings) throughout the cage, causing the keeper more work. Theoretically, some of these insects may be damaging to your house, should they escape the cage.

Chapter 5: Providing the Captive Habitat

Boas are capable climbers that often use branches when they are provided.

It is always advisable to sterilize branches before placing them in a cage. The easiest way to do so is by placing the branch in a 300-degree oven for about 15 minutes. Doing so should kill the vast majority of pests and pathogens lurking inside the wood.

Some keepers like to cover their branches with a water-sealing product. This is acceptable if a non-toxic product is used and the branches are allowed to air dry for several days before being placed in the cage. However, as branches are relatively easy and inexpensive to replace, it is not necessary to seal them if you plan to replace them.

You can attach the branches to the cage walls in many different ways. The branches should be held very securely, but you must be able to remove them periodically. This is not only necessary for routine cleaning and in the case of mite infestations, but removable branches are sometimes helpful when removing your animal from its cage – this is particularly true for small boas that spend most of their time on their perch. Instead of picking your boa up, simply lift the entire branch out, snake and all.

Closet rod holders are a popular choice, but they must not allow the branches to roll when the snake climbs on them. To keep them in a fixed position, small pegs can be placed on the branch ends

Chapter 5: Providing the Captive Habitat

that prevent them from rolling. Alternatively, branches with three or more ends can be used; three or more contact points prevent the branch from spinning.

Some keepers use hooks and eye-screws to suspend their branches. This method allows for quick and easy removal, but it is only applicable for cages with walls that will accept and support the eye-screws.

It can be challenging to suspend branches in glass cages and aquaria. It is often necessary to use an adhesive to hold the supports securely to the cage walls. This can be a problem if the adhesive loses strength and fails with your snake on top of it.

Another option is to make self-supporting structures for your boa to climb. This is often easy to accomplish with young boas, who way relatively little. Many branches can be placed in cages in such a way that they will support themselves. Use complex branches and trim them to fit the glass habitat. Usually, a large part of the branch should be on the cage floor to support its weight. Be careful placing pressure on glass walls or panels, as they crack easily.

Many different types of branches can be used in boa cages. Most non-aromatic hardwoods suffice. See the chart below for specific recommendations.

Whenever collecting wood to be used as cage props, bring a ruler so that you can visualize how large the branch will be, once it is back in the cage. Leave several inches of spare material at each end of the branch; this way, you can cut the perch to the correct length back home.

Always wash branches with plenty of hot water and a stiff, metal-bristled scrub brush to remove as much dirt, dust and fungus as possible before placing them in your boa's cage. Clean stubborn spots with a little bit of dish soap, but be sure to rinse them thoroughly afterwards.

Chapter 5: Providing the Captive Habitat

Recommended Species	Species to Avoid
Maple trees (*Acer* spp.)	**Cherry trees** (*Prunus* spp.)
Oak trees (*Quercus* spp.)	**Pine trees** (*Pinus* spp.)
Walnut trees (*Juglans* spp.)	**Cedar trees** (*Cedrus* spp., etc.)
Ash trees (*Fraxinus* spp.)	**Juniper trees** (*Juniperus* spp.)
Dogwood trees (*Cornus* spp.)	**Poison ivy / oak** (*Toxicodendron* spp.)
Sweetgum trees (*Liquidambar stryaciflua*)	
Crepe Myrtle trees (*Lagerstroemia* spp.)	
Tuliptrees (*Liriodendron tulipifera*)	
Pear trees (*Pyrus* spp.)	
Apple trees (*Malus* spp.)	
Manzanitas (*Arctostaphylos* spp.)	
Grapevine (*Vitis* spp.)	

Chapter 6: Maintaining the Captive Habitat

1) Cleaning Procedures

Once you have decided on the proper cage for your situation and pet, you must keep your snake fed, hydrated and ensure that the habitat stays in proper working order. This will require you to examine the cage daily to ensure that your snake is healthy and happy.

Some tasks must be completed each day, while others are should be performed weekly, monthly or annually.

Daily
- Monitor the ambient and surface temperatures of the habitat.
- Ensure that the snake's water bowl is full of clean water.
- Ensure that the snake has not defecated or produced urates in the cage. If he has, you must clean the cage.
- Ensure that the lights, latches and other moving parts are in working order.
- Verify that your snake is acting normally and appears healthy. You do not need to handle him to do so.
- Ensure that the humidity and ventilation are at appropriate levels.

Weekly
- Feed your snake (this may not be necessary each week).
- Empty, wash and refill the water container.
- Change the any sheet-like substrate.
- Clean the walls of the enclosure.
- Handle your snake (not after feeding time) and inspect him for any injuries, parasites or signs of illness.

Chapter 6: Maintaining the Captive Habitat

Monthly
- Break down the cage completely, remove and discard the substrate.
- Clean the entire cage from top to bottom.
- Sterilize the water dish and any other plastic or ceramic furniture in a mild bleach solution.
- Measure and weigh your snake
- Soak your snake for about 1 hour (Recommended, but not imperative).
- Photograph your snake (Recommended, but not imperative).

Annually
- Visit the veterinarian to ensure that your snake is in good health.
- Replace the batteries in your thermometers and any other devices that use them.

Cleaning a snake's cage or an item from his cage is relatively simple. Regardless of the way it became soiled or its constituent materials, the basic process is the same:

1. Rinse the object
2. Using a scrub brush or sponge and soapy water, remove any organic debris from the object.
3. Rinse the object thoroughly.
4. Disinfect the object.
5. Re-rinse the object.
6. Dry the object.

2) Chemicals & Tools

Scrub Brushes or Sponges
It helps to have a few different types of scrub brushes, sponges and similar tools. Use the least abrasive sponge or brush suitable for the task to prevent wearing out cage items prematurely. Do not use abrasive materials on glass or acrylic surfaces. Steel-

Chapter 6: Maintaining the Captive Habitat

bristled brushes work well for scrubbing wooden items, such as branches.

Soap
Use gentle, non-scented dish soap. Antibacterial soap is preferred, but not necessary. Most people use far more soap than is necessary -- a few drops mixed with a quantity of water is usually sufficient to help remove surface pollutants.

Bleach
Bleach (diluted to one-half cup per gallon of water) makes an excellent disinfectant. Be careful not to spill any on clothing, carpets or furniture, as it is likely to discolor the objects. Soak water bowls in this type of dilute bleach solution monthly. Always be sure to rinse objects thoroughly after using bleach and be sure that you cannot detect any residual odor. Bleach does not work as a disinfectant when in contact with organic substances; accordingly, the cage must be cleaned before you can disinfect it.

Veterinarian Approved Disinfectant
Many commercial products are available that are designed to be safe for their pets. Consult with your veterinarian about the best product for your situation, its method of use and its proper dilution.

Steam Cleaners
Steam cleaners are very effective for sterilizing cages, water bowls and durable cage props after they have been cleaned. Steam is a very effective for sterilizing surfaces, and it will not leave behind a toxic residue. Never use a steam cleaner near your snake or any other living creatures.

Avoid Phenols
Always avoid cleaners that contain phenols, as they are extremely toxic to snakes. In general, do not use household cleaning products to avoid exposing your pet to toxic chemicals.

Chapter 6: Maintaining the Captive Habitat

3) Keeping Records

It is important to keep records regarding your snake's health, feeding, shedding and other important details. In the past, snake keepers would do so on small index cards or in a notebook. In the modern world, technological solutions may be easier, such as using your computer or mobile device to keep track of the pertinent info about your snake.

While there is no limit to the amount of information you can record about your snake – and the more information to you record, the better. At a minimum, you should record the following:

Pedigree and Origin Information
Be sure to record the source of your pet, the date on which you acquired him and any other data that is available. If you purchase the snake from a quality breeder, you will likely be provided with information regarding the sire, dam, date of birth, weights and feeding records for the snake's entire life thus far.

Feeding Information
At a minimum, record the date and type of food item your snake eats at each feeding. If possible, record the time of day and weight of the food item as well. Additional notes may include techniques that were or were not successful, the prey species, and the color of the prey or any scenting techniques used. It is also helpful to record refused meals as well.

Shedding Information
It is only necessary to record the date of each shed, but it may also be helpful to record the date you notice the snake's eyes turning blue. Additionally, be sure to note any shedding difficulties. If you have to take steps to rectify a bad shed, note these as well. It is helpful to note when snakes turn blue, so you can anticipate when he will shed.

Chapter 6: Maintaining the Captive Habitat

Weights and Length

At a minimum, you should record the weight of your snake monthly or each time he sheds. Because you look at your snake frequently, it is important to track his weight to ensure he is growing properly. If you like, you can measure his length as well, but doing so is very difficult to produce accurate results. There are computer programs that will calculate the length of your snake if you photograph him near a ruler.

Maintenance Information

Record the dates and details of any major maintenance. For example, while it is not necessary to note that you topped off the water dish each day, it is appropriate to record the dates on which you change the substrate, or sterilize the cage.

Breeding Information

If you intend on breeding your snake, you should record all details regarding the pre=breeding conditioning, cycling, introductions, copulations, ovulation, pre-birth shed and birth.

Record all pertinent information about the litter as well, including number of viable offspring, stillborn young and unfertilized ova (called "slugs" by snake keepers).

Record Keeping Samples

The following are two different examples of suitable recording systems. The first example is reminiscent of the style of card that many breeders and experienced hobbyists use. Because such keepers often have numerous snakes, the notes are very simple, and require a minimum amount of writing or typing.

Note that in this example, the keeper has employed a simple code, so that he or she does not have to write out "fed this snake one small, thawed mouse."

Chapter 6: Maintaining the Captive Habitat

ID Number:	44522	Genus: Species/Sub:	Boa Constrictor ssp.	Gender: DOB:	Male 6/20/12	CARD #8
5.30.13 LM	6.07.13 LM	6.20.13 REFUSED LM	7.01.13 2 LM	7.08.13 LM		
6.03.13 SHED /350g	6.11.13 LM	6.22.13 REFUSED LM	7.04.13 REFUSED LM	7.13.13 LM		
6.04.13 LM	6.14.13 LM	6.30.13 SHED / 275g	7.05.13 LM			
SM= Small Mouse	MM= Medium Mouse	LM = Large Mouse				

The second example demonstrates a simple approach – keeping notes on paper – that is employed by many novice keepers. Such notes could be taken in a notebook or journal, or simply typed into a word processor. It does not ultimately matter how you keep records, just that you do keep records.

Date	Notes
6-22-13	*Acquired ""Feather Boa" the Suriname boa constrictor from a snake breeder named Mark at the in-town reptile expo. Mark explained that Feather's scientific name is Boa constrictor constrictor, but I can abbreviate it by writing: B. c. constrictor. Cost was $125. Mark was not sure what sex Solomon was, as he did not like to probe the young snakes. Mark said the snake was born last June, but he does not know the exact date. Feather is about 22-inches long.*
6-23-13	*I have decided to consider Feather a boy until I can get the vet to tell me what gender he really is. Feather spent the night in the container I bought him in, I purchased a 20-gallon aquarium, screened lid and heat lamp at the pet store. Bought the thermometer at the hardware store next door*

Chapter 6: Maintaining the Captive Habitat

	and ordered a non-contact thermometer online. I am using old food containers for his water dish and hide boxes.
6-27-13	*Feather shed today! He looks beautiful. Everything came off in one long piece.*
6-30-13	*I fed Feather a large thawed mouse today. I think I need longer tweezers! He was hungry!*
7-1-13	*Since Feather looked so hungry, I fed him another thawed mouse today.*
7-5-13	*Fed Feather one mouse. This one was brown, instead of white, but he didn't seem to care.*

Chapter 7: Feeding Captive Boa Constrictors

Boa constrictors are obligate carnivores that consume a wide variety of prey in the wild. This is good news for keepers, as most boas are enthusiastic eaters.

1) Live, Fresh Killed or Frozen

Whenever possible, snakes should be fed dead prey. Most often, this comes in the form of frozen-thawed rodents.

While boas are perfectly capable of killing and consuming small rodents, birds or lizards, these animals often fight back. If the snake does not grab its prey correctly, the creature may be free enough to bite or scratch the snake. Such bites can cause serious injuries to snakes, especially if they occur on the snake's head.

Additionally, it is far more humane for prey animal to be humanely euthanized than it is to be bitten, constricted and eaten by a snake.

Whenever thawing rodents, do so in warm water or at room temperature. Never attempt to thaw a rodent in the microwave.

2) Prey Species

In most circumstances, boas should be fed commercially raised rodents. However, captive produced chicks, ducks or rabbits will also suffice.

Some hobbyists offer their snakes a wider variety of food sources. While this may provide some small health benefits, many generations of snakes have been successfully raised solely on a diet of lab-raised rodents.

Chapter 7: Feeding Captive Boa Constrictors

Chicks are one potential alternative, although bird-eating snakes often produce soft, offensive smelling feces. Additionally, the chance of transmitting salmonella to your snakes by feeding them raw chicks is higher than it is with most other food sources.

Rabbits are an acceptable food source for boas that are large enough to eat them. Rabbits are widely available as frozen-thawed feeders.

3) Prey Size

The ability of boas to engulf large prey is legendary. In the wild, boas may eat large animals, including coatis, opossums and monkeys, but such large meals do present risks. Snakes may die from eating food that is too large, so err on the side of caution, and feed your boa prey that is between one and one-and-one-half times the snake's diameter at mid-body.

4) How to Offer Food

Always offer food to your snake when the room is calm and free of pets, rowdy children, and other distractions. Frightened or stressed snakes rarely eat. Additionally, feeding mistakes can be dangerous when dealing with large snakes.

Some snakes prefer to eat in low light conditions, while others may respond best during the middle of the day. The first step in feeding is to gather thawed, dry rodent and a pair of long forceps, tweezers or tongs. Then, open the cage door or remove the lid and set it aside.

Grab the food item with the forceps. Grip it behind the shoulder blades so that you can produce realistic movements with the item. Place the rodent's nose against a light bulb or in some very hot water for a few minutes to warm it up. Usually, the combination of the rodent odor and a good heat signature on the rodent's head is sufficient to elicit a strike. However, some snakes may be reluctant to eat unless the entire rodent is slightly warm.

Chapter 7: Feeding Captive Boa Constrictors

Move the food item about 3 or 4 inches in front of the snake's nose. If he is hungry and ready to eat, he may begin flicking his tongue. If so, you can gently place it closer to his face, wiggling it slightly.

Be patient, and allow the snake to gather his nerve and strike the food item. As soon as the snake strikes, try to release the mouse. With a bit of luck, the snake will constrict the rodent as if it were alive. Once this happens, slowly move back and out of the snake's line of sight.

Check on the snake in about five minutes, and be sure that he is still eating the rodent. (Do not leave the area where your snake is with the cage door open. If you can observe it from a distance, leave the door or lid open while backing away. If this will not be possible, try to close the cage as slowly as possible to prevent spooking the snake.)

Some snakes are prone to "forgetting" their dinner after they constrict it for a moment. This is usually not a big problem, as most snakes will accept the same rodent if re-offered. Some keepers have found that if you twitch the rodent slightly once the boa has constricted it (to simulate the struggles of the rodent) it may help keep the snake focused on the job.

If your snake does not begin tongue flicking when presented with the rodent, try to animate the rodent's movements a little. Wiggle it from left to right quickly and try to elicit tongue flicks.

Investigatory tongue flicks are different from causal, exploratory flicks. They are much more rapid, deliberate and the tongue often remains extended for a prolonged period of time.

If your movements do not generate any interest in the snake, gently move the rodent until it contacts the snake's nose gently. If successful, this may finally get the snake's attention, but often it will cause the snake to flee. If this happens, discard the rodent, replace the cage lid and try again in a day or two.

Chapter 7: Feeding Captive Boa Constrictors

Do not despair if your snake does not eat the first time you offer food. Many times, the snake may still be adjusting to his new home. Alternatively, he could be entering a shed cycle, during which time most snakes refuse food.

If your snake fails to eat after three different attempts, wait one full week before trying again. This should be enough time to allow him to shed or make it obvious that he is about to do so (opaque eyes, milky look to the skin).

5) Problem Feeders

It is not always possible to get a baby snake to begin accepting food voluntarily – this is when purchasing a snake from a reputable breeder pays off. Few breeders will sell their snakes before they are accepting food regularly and eagerly. If repeated attempts fail to yield positive results, you must take steps to jumpstart the process.

Once the snake refuses food for the fourth time (with at least one week elapsing to ensure shedding cycles are not the problem) contact the breeder, if you have not done so already.

Often, the breeder will be able to offer you tips or suggestions that may bring success. If you purchased the snake from a retail establishment, you can request suggestions, but substantial help is not as likely to follow.

6) Feeding Frequency

Most boas will thrive on a diet of one suitably sized rodent per week. For adults, this may even be excessive and cause them to gain weight. In general, most captive snakes are fed far more than they would eat in the wild.

Most snakes consume between two and four times their body mass per year (Rossi, 2006). Therefore, if you intend to feed your 1-pound snake once per week, each meal should be roughly 0.05 to .1 pounds, which is approximately the weight of a large adult mouse.

Chapter 7: Feeding Captive Boa Constrictors

7) Avoiding Regurgitation

If a snake is stressed or exposed to inappropriate temperatures, it may vomit any recently eaten food items. In addition to being a very unpleasant mess to clean up and a waste of money, vomiting is hard on the snake's body.

Many red-tailed boas (particularly young animals) are susceptible to chronic regurgitation, which leads to a downward spiral of health. It is important to understand that red-tailed boas are less forgiving of husbandry mistakes and should be fed less frequently than common boas are.

To avoid vomiting, always ensure your snake's habitat is the proper temperature, especially after eating. Additionally, refrain from handling your snake as long as a visible lump is present in his body. Even if the food item is too small to make a noticeable lump, refrain from handling a snake for at least 24 hours after feeding them.

If your snake vomits a food item, clean the cage immediately. Additionally, ensure that your snake can rehydrate properly. Many experienced keepers make it a practice to soak snakes after vomiting to ensure hydration.

Give snakes that vomit at least two full weeks before offering food again. One of the biggest mistakes keepers make when dealing with a snake that has regurgitated is that they try to make up for the lost meal too quickly. This is hard on the snake's digestive system and often causes long-term, chronic problems.

Chapter 8: Boa Constrictor Hydration

Like most other animals, boa constrictors require drinking water to remain healthy. However, the amount of water in the air (humidity) is an important factor in their health as well.

1) Humidity

Boa constrictors come from a wide range of habitats and locations – some live in equatorial rainforests, while others inhabit arid, subtropical lands. Accordingly, the ideal humidity level for your boa depends upon his subspecies and geographic origin.

As a rule of thumb, common and Argentine boas are comfortable at humidity levels of about 50 percent, while red-tailed boas and other species of the Amazon Basin thrive when kept at slightly higher humidity levels, around 60 percent.

However, fortunately for boa keepers, boas tolerate a wide range of humidity levels. Any of the subspecies will thrive when kept at moderate humidity levels. Boas should not be kept in dripping wet cages, nor should they be kept at very low humidity levels.

Most keepers will see fine results by simply incorporating a large water dish into the habitat. Cages with excess ventilation, such as many aquaria, may allow too much water to evaporate from the cage. Most problems occur as cages begin to dry out in the winter. Keepers living in very dry climates may need to increase the humidity level during these times.

Chapter 8: Boa Constrictor Hydration

2) Misting

One way to raise the humidity in the cage is by misting the substrate and interior surfaces of the enclosure with lukewarm water.

It is perfectly safe to spray your snake (gently) with clean, lukewarm water, but some do not like it. Avoid spraying a snake in the face – this often results in a defensive strike. Some snakes drink the droplets off their bodies after being misted.

Keepers with one snake will usually find a simple, handheld spray bottle to be sufficient. Keepers with many snakes are better served by acquiring a compressed-air sprayer.

Always allow the standing water droplets to evaporate or soak into the substrate between mistings – the cage should not stay wet for extended periods of time.

In addition to increasing the cage humidity temporarily, misting often causes boas to become active. This benefits them by encouraging exercise, mental stimulation, and, often, it causes them to defecate. Misting is also a stimulus used to elicit mating behavior.

One drawback to misting cages is that the water droplets can leave unsightly spots on glass surfaces. Water with a low-mineral content may help eliminate this possibility.

3) Drinking Water

Boa constrictors require regular access to clean, fresh water. Provide this by means of a small to medium-sized bowl or dish. While it is acceptable to offer the snakes a bowl that will accommodate the snake, be sure to avoid filling such containers too high, as they are apt to overflow if the snake crawls into the bowl.

However, this is not necessary, and many keepers use bowls with 2- to 4-inch diameters. Boas are muscular creatures that are apt to

Chapter 8: Boa Constrictor Hydration

tip their water bowl, so use a bowl heavy or wide enough that the snake will not tip it inadvertently.

Be sure to check the water dish daily and ensure that the water is clean. Empty, wash and refill the water dish any time it is contaminated with substrate, shed skin, urates or feces.

Some keepers prefer to use dechlorinated or bottled water for their snakes; however, untreated tap water is used by many keepers with no ill effects.

4) Soaking Water

In addition to providing drinking water, many keepers soak their boas periodically in a tub of clean, lukewarm water. Soaking is helpful tool for the husbandry of many snakes, including boas, who often hail from very wet habitats. In addition to ensuring that your snake remains adequately hydrated, soaks help to remove dirt and encourage complete, problem-free sheds. It is not necessary to soak your snake if it remains adequately hydrated, but most boas benefit from an occasional soak.

Soaks should last a maximum of about one hour, and be performed no more often than once per week (unless the snake is experiencing shedding difficulties).

When soaking your snake, the water should not be very deep. Never make your snake swim to keep its head above water. Ideally, snakes should be soaked in containers with only enough water to cover their back. This should allow your snake to rest comfortably with its head above water.

Never leave a snake unattended while it is soaking.

Chapter 8: Boa Constrictor Hydration

5) Common Husbandry Problems and Solutions

Problem	Solution
Cage too cool	• Increase power / wattage of heating devices • Add additional heating devices • Place heating devices closer to the cage • Incorporate more thermal mass in the cage • Insulate the cage • Reduce the ventilation slightly • Move the cage to a different location
Cage too warm	• Reduce power / wattage of heating devices • Remove some of the heating devices • Use a rheostat / thermostat to reduce temperature • Remove thermal mass from the cage • Move cage to a different location
Cage too dry	• Mist the cage more frequently / thoroughly • Increase the size of the water dish • Use moisture-retaining substrate • Reduce ventilation slightly • Add live plants to the enclosure • Use bubbler in water dish
Cage too damp	• Increase ventilation • Swap live plants for artificial plants • Reduce the size of the water dish • Allow substrate to dry before adding to the cage

Chapter 8: Boa Constrictor Hydration

Problem	Solution
Incomplete sheds	- Increase cage humidity - Include a humid hide box - Implement a soaking regimen - Avoid handling snake during shed cycles - Ensure the snake has no health problems (mites, etc.)
Snake doesn't eat	- Try feeding at a different time of day - Experiment with different food items (mice, chicks, rats) - Experiment with different food presentations - Assess cage temperatures, ensure they are correct - Reduce the snake's stress -- less handling, more hides
Snake cage smells	- Clean the cage more often / thoroughly - Switch to paper substrate - Increase cage ventilation
Snake pacing cage	- Ensure cage temperatures are not too high - Ensure snake has water - Ensure the snake has an adequate number of hides - Mature males may be searching for female
Snake is aggressive	- Ensure the cage is not subject to vibration, etc. - Ensure the cage features enough hiding opportunities - Ensure temperatures are correct

Chapter 8: Boa Constrictor Hydration

- Reduce handling frequency

Chapter 9: Interacting with Pet Boa Constrictors

1) Handling

One of the most enjoyable aspects of snake keeping for many people is handling their pet. While most boa constrictors learn to accept regular, gentle handling, proper technique will make handling time more enjoyable for you and less stressful for your pet.

2) Picking up a Snake

Learning to pick up a snake correctly is easy, and will often yield positive results, as it starts handling sessions on the right track.

1. Ensure the surroundings are conducive to snake handling. Do not pick up snakes (unless necessary) when pets, children or other potential distractions are nearby.
2. Open the cage or take off the lid.
3. Immediately scoop your hand under the snake and gently lift him around the middle of his body.
4. With your other hand, support the rest of his body and remove him from the cage.

Do not stand in front of the cage for extended periods of time, trying to gather the nerve to pick up your snake. This often makes snakes nervous. The goal is for your snake to learn to anticipate the activity and react calmly.

If the snake shows signs of aggression, you should remain deliberate and calm. Many young boas are feisty as youngsters, but their strikes and bites are harmless. With repeated handling sessions, such snakes usually become considerably tamer.

Chapter 9: Interacting with Pet Boa Constrictors

It is important to consider that some snakes may never become tractable, trustworthy pets. You will still need to care for your snake if this happens, and you need to have a plan of action for doings so.

Many advanced keepers would simply proceed as usual, and simply endure the mildly irritating bites and strikes. However, beginners will often feel better using alternative methods to handle aggressive snakes.

3) How to Hold a Snake

When holding a snake, avoid restraining it. Instead, seek to support its body weight, and allow it to crawl from one hand to the other. It is always wise to handle the snake over a table or other object to prevent his from falling to the floor, should he make a sudden move.

Always realize that you are responsible for your snake while you are holding it. Accidents can and have happened. Such occurrences are very bad for snakes, snake keepers and the entire snake-keeping hobby, and must be avoided. Never handle your snake in a public situation.

Do not take your snake to the park or to the local fast food restaurant. Your snake is not a toy, he does not appreciate "hanging out" in this manner, and it makes snake keepers everywhere look bad.

Snakes frighten many people and you should always be sensitive to this fact. Rather than playing into these fears, seek to educate people about snakes rather than shock them by bringing them to inappropriate events and locations.

4) Safely Handling Large Boas

Even when completely tame, large boas are challenging to handle. A 50-pound boa is an incredibly strong animal that can be dangerous, should it become spooked or frightened. Accordingly, boas in excess of about 6 or 7 feet in length should only be handled with another person present.

Always be sure to avoid smelling like potential prey when handling large boas. While a defensive bite can cause damage, a feeding-response bite is much more likely to cause serious injury. The boa is likely to constrict after striking, which can cause further injuries and make it more difficult to extract the snake's teeth from your skin and end the encounter.

Be sure to change your clothes and wash your hands thoroughly after handling rodents, birds or other pets. Never handle a large boa in the presence of children or pets.

Additionally, as boas may be more aggressive and active during low-light conditions, it is safer to handle them during the day, with the lights on.

5) Dealing with Aggressive Snakes

Unfortunately, just as with dogs, cats and humans, some boas have defensive personalities. Fortunately, with regular, gentle handling, most young boas outgrow this attitude, although many never become completely trustworthy. A small percentage do not calm down, despite the consistent efforts of the keeper.

Young, defensive boas may bite the hand that holds them, but their bites are essentially harmless.

The Paper Towel Trick
When you open the snake's cage, place a paper towel (or piece of newspaper or clean cloth) over him. Then, pick him and the paper up in one smooth motion. Usually, by placing the newspaper over the snake, it will refrain from biting.

The Flat Hand Trick
Similar to the paper towel trick, the flat hand trick relies on covering the snake quickly. The difference is that in this case, you use your hand to cover the snake. Quickly and gently, lay your flat hand over the snake, trying to cover him completely. Using

your thumb, scoop him up and place him in your other hand or in a temporary container.

Part of the beauty of the flat hand trick is that it is hard for a young boa to open its mouth wide enough to bite a flat surface effectively. They may stills strike, and may even puncture the skin, but the bites are generally minor.

The flat hand technique is unsuitable for boas that are not small enough to fit under your flattened hand. The boa must be laying in a flat coil for this method to work well.

The Hook Trick
By using a small snake hook or bent coat hanger to lift a snake, they often remain calmer than using your hand. Once on the hook, the snake can be placed in your hand or in a temporary container. Be sure to use a hook that is smooth and has no sharp edges that may injure the snake.

6) In The Event of a Bite

If your boa bites you, remain calm. Most defensive bites involve a quick strike-bite-release, whereas feeding mistakes usually cause the boa to hold on and potentially begin constricting.

If it is a defensive bite, and the snake releases its hold, close the cage or return the snake to his enclosure. Then, wash the wound thoroughly with soap and warm water. Consult your doctor if the bite is serious, will not stop bleeding or you can feel teeth lodged in the wound. If the snake does not release his grip, the best thing to do is place him in a bucket of cold water. Alternatively, you can hold him under cold, running water.

Wash the wound, and contact your doctor.

7) Temporary Transport Cages

The best way to transport your snake is with a plastic storage container. The container must have ample air holes to allow ventilation and it must be safe and secure.

Chapter 9: Interacting with Pet Boa Constrictors

Some keepers prefer transparent boxes for such purposes, as they allow you to see the snake while it is inside the box. This is definitely a benefit – especially when opening and closing the box – but opaque transportation boxes provide your snake with more security, as they cannot see the activity going on outside their container.

Place a few paper towels or some clean newspaper in the bottom of the box to give your snake somewhere to hide and to absorb any fluids, should your snake defecate or discharge urates.

8) Transporting Tips

When traveling with your snake, pay special attention to the temperature. Use the air-conditioning or heater in your vehicle to keep the snake within his comfortable range (the mid-70s Fahrenheit are ideal in most circumstances).

Do not jostle your snake unnecessarily, nor leave it unattended in a car. Make sure that the transport container is secure – in the unfortunate circumstance in which you are in an accident, a loose snake is not an additional problem with which you need to contend.

Do not take your snake with you on public transportation.

9) Hygiene

Always practice good hygiene when handling snakes. Wash your hands with soap and warm water each time you touch your snake, his habitat or the tools you use to care for him.

Never wash cages or tools in kitchens or bathrooms that are used by humans.

Chapter 10: Common Health Concerns

Unlike humans, who can tell you when they are sick, snakes endure illness stoically. This does not mean that injury or illnesses do not cause them distress, but without expressive facial features, they do not look like they are suffering.

In fact, many snake illnesses do not produce symptoms until the disease has already reached an advanced state. Accordingly, it is important to treat injuries and illness promptly to provide your pet with the best chance of recovery.

Acquiring competent veterinary care for a tropical snake is not as easy as finding a veterinarian to treat a dog or cat. Those living in major metropolitan areas are likely to find one reasonably close, but rural snake keepers may have to take great lengths to find a suitable vet.

1) Finding a Suitable Veterinarian

Relatively few veterinarians treat snakes and other reptiles. It is important to find a snake-oriented veterinarian before you need one. There are a number of ways to do this:

- You can search veterinarian databases to find one that is local and treats reptiles.
- You can inquire with your dog or cat veterinarian to see if he or she knows a qualified reptile-oriented veterinarian to whom he or she can refer you.
- You can contact a local reptile-enthusiast group or club. Most such organizations will be familiar with the local veterinarians.

Chapter 10: Common Health Concerns

- You can inquire with local nature preserves or zoos. Most such institutions have relationships with veterinarians that treat reptiles and other exotic animals.

If you happen to live in a remote area and do not have a reptile-oriented veterinarian within driving distance, you can try to find a conventional veterinarian who will treat your animal after consulting with a reptile-oriented veterinarian. Such visits may be expensive, as you will have to pay for two veterinary visits (the actual visit and the phone consultation), but it may be your only choice.

2) Reasons to Visit the Veterinarian

While snakes do not require vaccinations or similar routine treatments, they may require visits for other reasons. Anytime your snake exhibits signs of illness or suffers an injury, you must visit the veterinarian.

Visit your veterinarian when:

- You first acquire your snake. This will allow your veterinarian to familiarize himself or herself with your pet while it is presumably healthy. This gives him or her a baseline against which he or she can consider future deviations. Additionally, your veterinarian may be able to diagnose existing illnesses, before they cause serious problems.
- Your time your snake wheezes, exhibits labored breathing or produces a mucus discharge from its nostrils or mouth.
- Your snake produces soft or watery feces. (Soft feces are expected when snakes are fed some food items, such as birds. This is not necessarily cause for concern.)
- Your snake suffers any significant injury. Common examples include thermal burns, friction damage to the rostral (nose) region or damaged scales.

Chapter 10: Common Health Concerns

- Reproductive issues occur, such as being unable to deliver young. If a snake appears nervous, agitated or otherwise stressed and unable to give birth, see your veterinarian immediately.
- Your snake fails to feed for an extended period. While many snakes fast from time to time – which is no cause for concern – new snakes that do not eat for 4 weeks should be seen by a veterinarian. Snakes that have been in your care, and normally eat aggressively, may fast for longer than this without ill effects.

3) Common Health Problems

Some of the common health problems, their causes and suggested course of action follow.

Retained or Poor Sheds

Captive snakes – especially in the hands of novice keepers – often shed poorly. With proper husbandry, healthy snakes should produce one-piece sheds regularly (if the shed skin is broken in one or two places, but comes off easily, there is no cause for concern).

Retained sheds can cause health problems, particularly if they restrict blood flow. This is often a problem when a snake retains a bit of old skin near the tail tip.

If your snake sheds poorly, you must take steps to remove the old skin and review your husbandry to prevent the problem from happening again. If you are providing ideal husbandry parameters, and yet your snake still experiences poor sheds, consult your veterinarian to rule out illness.

The best way to remove retained sheds is by soaking your snake or placing him in a damp container for about an hour. After removing him, see if you can gently peel the skin off. Try to keep the skin in as few pieces as possible to make the job easier.

Do not force the skin off your snake. If it does not come off easily, return him to his cage and repeat the process again in 12 to

Chapter 10: Common Health Concerns

24 hours. Usually, repeated soaks or time in a damp hide will loosen the skin sufficiently to be removed.

If repeated treatments do not yield results, consult your veterinarian. He may feel that the retained shed is not causing a problem, and advise you to leave it attached – it should come off with the snake's next shed. Alternatively, it if is causing a problem, the veterinarian can remove it without much risk of harming your snake.

Retained Spectacles
Unlike a simple retained shed, a retained spectacle (eye cap) is a serious matter. Do not try to remove a retained spectacle yourself; simply keep the snake in a humid environment and take it to your veterinarian, who should be able to remove it relatively easily.

Respiratory Infections
Like humans, snakes can suffer from respiratory infections. Snakes with respiratory infections exhibit fluid or mucus draining from their nose and/or mouth, may be lethargic and are unlikely to eat. They may also spend excessive amounts of time basking on or under the heat source, in an effort to induce a "behavioral fever."

Bacteria, or, less frequently, fungi or parasites often cause respiratory infections. In addition, cleaning products, perfumes, pet dander and other particulate matter can irritate a snake's respiratory tract as well. Some such bacteria are ubiquitous, and only become problematic when they overwhelm a snake's immune system. Other bacteria (and most viruses) are transmitted from one snake to another. To reduce the chances of illnesses, keep your snake quarantined from other snakes, keep his enclosure exceptionally clean and be sure to provide the best husbandry possible, in terms of temperature and humidity. Additionally, avoid stressing your snake by handling him too frequently, or exposing him to chaotic situations.

Upon taking your snake to the vet, he or she will likely take samples of the mucus and have them analyzed to determine the causal agent. The veterinarian will then prescribe medications, if appropriate, such as antibiotics.

It is imperative to carry out the actions prescribed by your veterinarian exactly as stated, and keep your snake's stress level very low while he is healing. Stress can reduce immune function, so avoid handling him unnecessarily, and consider covering the front of his cage while he recovers.

Many snakes produce audible breathing sounds for a few days immediately preceding a shed cycle. This is rarely cause for concern and will resolve once the snake sheds. However, if you are in doubt, always seek veterinary attention.

"Mouth Rot"
Mouth rot – properly called stomatitis – is identified by noting discoloration, discharge or cheesy-looking material in the snake's mouth. Mouth rot can be a serious illness, and requires the attention of your veterinarian.

While mouth rot can follow an injury (such as happens when a snake strikes the side of a glass cage) it can also arise from systemic illness. Your veterinarian will cleanse your snake's mouth and potentially prescribe an antibiotic. Your veterinarian may recommend withholding food until the problem is remedied. Always be sure that snakes recovering from mouth rot have immaculately clean habitats, with ideal temperatures.

Internal Parasites
In the wild, most snakes carry some internal parasites. While it may not be possible to keep a snake completely free of internal parasites, it is important to keep these levels in check.

Consider any wild-caught snake to be parasitized until proven otherwise. While most captive bred snakes should have relatively few internal parasites, they can suffer from such problems as well.

Preventing parasites from building to pathogenic levels requires strict hygiene. Many parasites build up to dangerous levels when

Chapter 10: Common Health Concerns

the snakes are kept in a cage that is continuously contaminated from feces.

Most internal parasites that are of importance for snakes are transmitted via the fecal-oral route. This means that eggs (or a similar life stage) of the parasites are released with the feces. If the snake inadvertently ingests these, the parasites can develop inside the snake's body and cause increased problems. Such eggs are usually microscopic and easily lifted into the air, where they may stick to cage walls or land in the water dish. Later, when the snake flicks its tongue or drinks from the water dish, it ingests the eggs.

Internal parasites may cause your snake to vomit, pass loose stools, and fail to grow or refuse food entirely. Other parasites may produce no symptoms at all, demonstrating the importance of routine examinations.

Your veterinarian will usually examine your snake's feces if he suspects internal parasites. By looking at the type of eggs inside the snake's feces, you veterinarian can prescribe an appropriate medication. Many parasites are easily treated with anti-parasitic medications, but often, these medications must be given several times to eradicate the pathogens completely.

Some parasites may be transmissible to people, so always take proper precautions, including regular hand washing and keeping snakes and their cages away from kitchens and other areas where foods are prepared. Examples of common internal parasites include roundworms, tapeworms and amoebas.

External Parasites
The primary external parasites that afflict snakes are ticks and snake mites. Ticks are rare on captive bred animals, but wild caught snakes often have a few.

Ticks should be removed manually. Using tweezers grasp the tick as close as possible to the snake's skin and pull with steady, gentle pressure. Do not place anything over the tick first, such as petroleum jelly, or carry out any other "home remedies," such as

Chapter 10: Common Health Concerns

burning the tick with a match. Such techniques may cause the tick to inject more saliva (which may contain diseases or bacteria) into the snake's body.

Drop the tick in a jar of isopropyl alcohol to ensure it is killed. It is a good idea to bring these to your veterinarian for analysis. Do not contact ticks with your bare hands, as many species can transmit disease to humans.

Mites are another matter entirely. While ticks are generally large enough to see easily, mites are about the size of a pepper flake. Whereas tick infestations usually only tally a few individuals, mite infestations may include thousands of individual parasites.

Mites may afflict wild caught snakes, but, as they are not confined to a small cage, such infestations are somewhat self-limiting. However, in captivity, mite infestations can approach plague proportions.

After a female mite feeds on a snake, she drops off and finds a safe place (such as a tiny crack in a cage or among the substrate) to deposit her eggs. After the eggs hatch, they travel back to your snake (or to other snakes in your collection) where they feed and perpetuate the lifecycle.

Whereas a few mites may represent little more than an inconvenience to the snake, a significant infection stresses them considerably, and may even cause death through anemia. This is particularly true for small or young animals. Additionally, mites may transmit disease from one snake to another.

There are a number of different methods for eradicating a mite infestation. In each case, there are two primary steps that must be taken: You must eradicate the snake's parasites, as well as the parasites in the snake's environment (which includes the room in which the cage resides).

It is relatively simple to remove mites from a snake. When mites get wet, they die. However, mites are protected by a thick, waxy exoskeleton that encourages the formation of an air bubble. This

Chapter 10: Common Health Concerns

means that you cannot place your snake in water to drown the mites. The mites will simply hide under the snake's scales, using their air bubble to protect themselves.

To defeat this waxy cuticle, all that is needed is a few drops of gentle dish soap added to the water. The soap will lower the surface tension of water, allowing it to penetrate under the snake's scales. Additionally, the soap disrupts the surface tension of the water, preventing the air bubble from forming.

By soaking your snake is the slightly soapy water for about one hour will kill most of the mites on his body. Use care when doing so, but try to arrange the water level and container so that most of the snake's body is below the water.

While the snake is soaking, perform a thorough cage cleaning. Remove everything from the cage, including water dishes, substrates and cage props. Sterilize all impermeable cage items, and discard the substrate and all porous cage props. Vacuum the area around the cage and wipe down all of the nearby surfaces with a wet cloth.

It may be necessary to repeat this process several times to eradicate the mites completely. Accordingly, the very best strategy is to avoid contracting mites in the first place. This is why it is important to purchase your snake from a reliable breeder or retailer, and keep your snake quarantined from potential mite vectors. As an example, even if you purchase your snake from a reliable source, provide excellent husbandry and clean the cage regularly, you can end up battling mites if your friend brings his snake – which has a few mites – to your house.

It may be possible for mites to crawl onto your hands or clothes, hop off when you return home and make their way to your snake. This is why many breeders and experienced hobbyists avoid visiting low-quality pet stores or places with poorly tended snake cages. While it is relatively easy to observe mites on a snake that has a significant infestation, a few mites may go unnoticed. Make it a practice to inspect your snake and his cage regularly. Look in

Chapter 10: Common Health Concerns

the crease under the snake's lower jaw, near the eyes and near the vent; all of these are places in which mites hide. It can also be helpful to wipe down your snake with a damp, white paper towel. After wiping down the snake, observe the towel to see if any mites are present.

Chemical treatments are also available to combat mites, but you must be very careful with such substances. Beginners should rely on their veterinarian to prescribe or suggest the appropriate chemicals.

Avoid repurposing lice treatments or other chemicals, as is often encouraged by other hobbyists. Such non-intended use may be very dangerous, and it is often in violation of Federal laws.

New hobbyists should consult with their veterinarian if they suspect that their snake has mites. Mite eradication is often a challenging ordeal that your veterinarian can help make easier.

Long-Term Anorexia
While short-term fasts of one to two weeks are common among snakes, fasts that last longer than this may be cause for concern. If your snake refuses food, ensure that its habitat is set up ideally with ample hiding opportunities and access to appropriate temperatures.

If none of these factors are inappropriate, and therefore likely to be causing the problem, consult your veterinarian. Above all, do not panic – snakes can go very long periods of time without food. Your veterinarian will want to make sure that your snake is in good health, as respiratory infections or internal parasites may cause it to refuse food.

Some snakes refuse food in the winter, as would happen in the wild. While you should consult with your veterinarian the first time this happens, subsequent refusals during the winter do not usually indicate a problem.

Mouth rot, respiratory illness and parasites can cause snakes to refuse food.

Chapter 11: Color Variations

Chapter 11: Color Variations

Occasionally, a strange-looking boa is captured from the wild, or emerges serendipitously from a captive female. Sometimes, this strange appearance is merely the result of individual variation; in other cases, the strange appearance is shown to be predictably inherited, via a genetic mutation.

Some of these mutations (often called "morphs" in the boa hobby) are only slightly different from normal-looking boas, while others appear like snakes from a different planet. These unique animals may survive in captivity, but in the wild, most would quickly be eaten by predators, without their cryptic color patterns.

Many of these color variations are very expensive, but as the supply increases, the price falls. In many cases, some of the earliest established mutations are near the same price as normal-looking animals.

1) Patterns of Inheritance

Different mutations are inherited in different ways.

Snakes receive one copy of each gene from their mother and one from their father. Some genes affect the animal's appearance when only one copy is present, while others require two copies of a gene to express the associated trait.

When an animal has two copies of the same gene, it is said to be homozygous. When an animal has one copy of a mutant gene and one copy of the normal gene, it is called heterozygous.

Chapter 11: Color Variations

Simple Recessive
Simple recessive traits are only expressed when an animal has two copies of the mutant gene. However, normal looking, but heterozygous animals may produce offspring that display the trait associated with the gene, if the other parent has a copy of the gene as well.

Dominant

Dominant traits are expressed whenever they are present, regardless of the other gene in the pair. Accordingly, dominant traits become very common in a given gene pool. The natural "wild" appearance of boas is dominant over most genes, although some genes, such as the arabesque trait, dominate the wild appearance.

There is no visual difference between an animal with one copy of the gene or two copies of the gene. However, a dominant animal that is homozygous for the mutation only produces young that display the morph.

Incompletely Dominant
Incompletely dominant mutations are similar to dominant mutations except that those with one copy of the gene look different than those with two copies of the mutant gene do.

Often, homozygous animals have a more extreme version of the color or pattern mutation, than heterozygous animals do.

Often, incompletely dominant mutations are called co-dominant mutations. However, this terminology is not technically correct. Animals that display co-dominant traits exhibit a combination of two or more genes.

Polygenetic Traits
Some traits, like pattern and ground color, are influenced by a group of genes. Such traits are typically expressed best in selectively bred lines. Polygenetic traits are not inherited in a predictable fashion.

Chapter 11: Color Variations

2) Color Mutations

New mutations are found constantly, but the following are a few of the most common types.

"Albinos"
When snake keepers discuss "albino" snakes, they are really referring to amelanistic animals. A true "albino" animal produces no pigment, while an amelanistic animal fails to produce melanin. Melanin is the pigment responsible for brown, gray and black color in snakes. Additionally it is also responsible for darkening other colors, such as red and yellow.

Historically, there were two primary types of boa referred to as "albino." One is called the "Kahl" line and the other is called the "Sharp" line, both of which are named after the breeders that established them in the hobby. Both are simple-recessive mutations that only manifest in the animal's phenotype if two copies of the mutant gene occur in the same animal. The two types are not compatible – meaning that they do not work in conjunction with each other. A "Kahl" albino bred to a "Sharp" albino produces normal-looking young that have one copy of the gene for each mutation.

There are thought to be two primary types of albinism that occur in boas: Animals with one type of the mutation – called tyrosinase positive – produce a chemical involved in the production of dark pigment, while those with the other type – called tyrosinase negative – do not produce the chemical.

The presence or lack of tyrosinase drastically effects the appearance of albinos. The "classic" albino (which resembles the "Kahl" line) is thought to be tyrosinase negative. Such animals are largely yellow and white, and they have relatively little contrast.

By contrast, those thought to be tyrosinase positive are much darker. Over the last few years, several different examples of this mutation have been discovered. They vary greatly in appearance, although most of the lines are compatible with each other. However, the resulting offspring may look slightly different than either of the parents.

When one of the purported tyrosinase positive boas was bred to a "Sharp" albino, an interesting thing happened – the resulting clutch contained animals that looked like "Sharp" albinos. After much examination, many began to suspect that the "Sharp" albinos are actually tyrosinase positive, they just have exhibit an extreme (and beautiful) version of the gene, in which the majority of the dark coloration is lost.

If this is true, it means that as of the publication date, there is only one form of tyrosinase negative albino boa – the "Kahl" line.

All forms of amelanism in boas are inherited in simple recessive fashion.

Hypomelanistic
Hypomelanistic animals display reduced, but not absent, levels of melanin. Many look "faded" or "washed out." This reduction of pigment, can make the animals appear very sharp and crisp, with little dark speckling.

There are two primary hypomelanistic lines, and both are inherited in incomplete dominant fashion.

Blood Boas
Blood boas have a very reddish color as neonates and become rich orange-colored as adults. The trait is inherited in simple recessive fashion.

Anerythristic
Anerythristic boas lack the ability to produce red pigments. As babies, most anerythristic boas are gray and black snakes, although the adults tend to become brownish. Anerythrism is inherited in simple recessive fashion.

3) Pattern Mutations

Some pattern mutations also affect the color of a boa as well.

Chapter 11: Color Variations

Motley Boas
Motley boas look darker than normal boas and have a reduced pattern. An incomplete dominant mutation, the homozygous form of the morph is a largely black animal.

Arabesque
The Arabesque mutation was one of the first mutations established by boa breeders. Arabesque boas have connected dorsal patterns and increased black speckling on the light-colored pattern elements.

The Arabesque mutation is dominant, meaning that homozygous individuals appear identical to heterozygous animals. There are two different lines of the mutation.

Below is a synopsis of a few of the most common color and pattern mutations. New morphs are established continually, and this list is far from exhaustive.

Mutation	Pattern of Inheritance
Normal	Dominant
Amelanistic / Albino	Simple Recessive
Anerythristic	Simple Recessive
Blood	Simple Recessive
Hypomelanistic	Incomplete Dominant
Caramel (VPI)	Simple Recessive
Caramel (Boawoman Hypo)	Simple Recessive
Coral Albino	Unknown
Leopard	Simple Recessive
Leucistic	Incomplete Dominant
Prodigy	Simple Recessive
Squaretail	Unknown
Arabesque	Dominant
Salmon	Incomplete Dominant
Jungle	Incomplete Dominant
Maroon	Incomplete Dominant
Motley	Incomplete Dominant

Chapter 11: Color Variations

Blonde T+ Albino	Simple Recessive
Key West	Incomplete Dominant
Aztec	Incomplete Dominant

4) Mutation Combinations

Breeders have produced a number of boas that bear more than one genetic mutation. For example, some boas have one of the albino genes and a hypomelanistic gene.

The number of possible combinations are mind blowing; while some pattern and color mutations do not work well together, others combine to produce incredibly beautiful snakes.

An example of the motley pattern mutation

One example of a mutation combination called the "snow morph" or "snow mutation" relies on the albino gene to remove most of the black from a boa, while the anerythristic gene removes the red tones from the animal. The result is an animal that is almost completely white and yellow.

However, the process by which snow boas are produced is more complicated than it is to produce a boa with only one trait.

To produce a snow boa, breeders pair an albino boa with an anerythristic boa. The resulting offspring all look normal, but carry one copy of each gene mutation.

Chapter 11: Color Variations

When these offspring mature, they are bred together. Statistically, one in sixteen of the resulting babies will have two copies of each recessive gene, thereby producing a snow boa. The other 15 snakes form a combination of anerythristic, albino and normal appearing snakes. Some of the young will carry one copy of one of the mutated genes. Additionally, one of the 16 babies will be completely normal, and carry none of the mutant genes.

Some of the common color combinations are detailed in the chart below:

Name	Combination
Blizzard	Anerythristic x Hypo
Ghost	Anerythristic x Hypo
Paradigm	Sharp Albino x Boawoman Caramel
Snow	Albino x Anerythristic
Sunglow	Sharp Albino x Hypo
Snowglow	Sharp Albino x Hypo x Anerythristic

Notice the red eyes and lack of dark scales on this albino boa.

Chapter 12: Breeding Boa Constrictors

Chapter 12: Breeding Boa Constrictors

1) Determining Gender

Boas are somewhat easier to sex than many other snakes as adults. Mature males possess much larger cloacal spurs than females do – generally, those of the female require effort to find, while those of males are obvious. Males use these spurs to stimulate females before breeding.

Additionally, females grow to much larger sizes than males do. In practice, this is only valuable for distinguishing females. In other words, any boa exceeding 8 feet in length or 20 pounds in weight is likely a female. While this is a reasonably accurate method for determining the gender of large females, it is not 100 percent reliable.

2) Pre-Breeding Considerations

Before you set out to breed your boas, consider the decision carefully. Few people realize all of the implications of breeding before they set out to do so.

Ask yourself if you will be able to:

- Provide the proper care for the female while gravid
- Afford emergency veterinary services if necessary
- Provide housing for up to 60 babies
- Provide food for up to 60 babies
- Dedicate the time to establishing up to 60 babies
- Find the time to care for up to 60 babies
- Find new homes for up to 60 babies
- Afford to heat up to 60 baby snake habitats

Few people are able to do all of these things. While it is unlikely that your boa will have a litter of 60 babies, it is possible, and you must be prepared to deal with this.

Many people see the price tags associated with many snakes, and instantly envision themselves becoming snake breeders. However, the vast majority of people that try to breed snakes for profit fail.

Becoming a snake breeder means that you may have to obtain licenses, insurance or permits to do so legally, depending on your area.

3) Pre-Breeding Conditioning

Snakes should be well fed, but not obese, before breeding. Some keepers increase the amount of food offered to females prior to cycling, but others feel that the standard diet is sufficient. In most cases, captive snakes eat more food than their wild counterparts do, so typical feeding schedules are adequate.

4) Cycling

Cycling is a technique used to breed many snake species. Cycling typically refers to establishing a yearly temperature and light cycle. In many snake species, cycling is necessary for successful breeding. However, it does not appear that cycling is necessary for boa constrictors.

There are a wide variety of approaches employed by boa breeders – some engage in typical cycling techniques, others use only mild cycling strategies and others avoid cycling their snakes at all.

It is likely that there are some subtle changes that occur throughout the year, despite the breeder's attempts to keep the conditions consistent. However, such changes are likely very negligible.

Those keepers who do cycle their animals usually drop the nighttime temperatures during the fall or winter.

Chapter 12: Breeding Boa Constrictors

5) Pairing

Most North American breeders pair boas in the fall. However, some pairs may court for extended periods of time before they breed.

Because female boas should be disturbed as little as possible during the gestation process, it is best to place the male in the female's cage.

Observe the pair closely after placing them together to ensure that they are not acting antagonistically towards each other. It is rare for a male-female pair to fight, but if it does occur, you must separate the snakes immediately to prevent serious injuries.

Copulation rarely begins right after the male and female are introduced to each other. It usually takes several hours to days for the male to begin courting the female.

Some keepers elect to separate the male and female periodically throughout the breeding season, while others leave the males and females together until ovulation is witnessed.

6) Eliciting Copulation

Occasionally, males fail to court and breed the female with whom they are paired. Sometimes, there is nothing that can be done to change this – some pairs are simply not compatible. However, boa breeders have devised a number of techniques over the years that may help encourage copulation.

Boas often form breeding aggregations in the wild, consisting of a single female and several males. The presence of other males may incite the male's competitive instincts, and cause him to breed.

While you can use another live male boa to accomplish this, there is a small chance that the males will combat with each other. Often, placing the shed skin of another male in the cage with the pair is effective without putting the males at risk.

Chapter 12: Breeding Boa Constrictors

If you do not have another male or shed skin to use (or you have tried such techniques unsuccessfully), it may be helpful to scratch the male near his spurs, back and vent area. This is thought to simulate the feeling caused by another male's spurs, which may spark his competitive instincts.

Some boa breeders have noticed that copulation often occurs during thunderstorms. While you cannot control the weather, you can certainly take advantage of storms when they occur. If possible, open the windows to lower the barometric pressure in the room. Misting the snakes with water may also encourage breeding activity.

If you have tried every method possible to elicit breeding activity, and had no success, separate the animals and wait for one of them to shed. Place the animals back together immediately after the shed and hope for the best.

Ultimately, some pairs are just incompatible. In such cases there is little the keeper can do except try to switch animals and hope for better chemistry with a new pair.

7) Gestation

Gestation takes 125 days from the date of ovulation. Usually, the boas shed their skin about 105 days before giving birth.

Do not disturb a gravid boa unless absolutely necessary. Some keepers withhold food while gravid, while others feed their boa a few meals. If food is offered, it should be smaller than normal to prevent complicating the gestation.

8) Parturition

Some keepers have noticed that boas often give birth during rainstorms. This may have an adaptive value, as the birth site becomes covered in bodily fluids, which likely attracts predators. By giving birth in the rain, many of these fluids are washed away.

Chapter 12: Breeding Boa Constrictors

Some keepers prefer to remove the young immediately after the female has finished giving birth, while others prefer to give them a few days to rest before going in to remove them.

Always be cautious when trying to remove the babies from the mother – mothers are often very defensive at this time.

9) Neonatal Husbandry

When the young are first removed from the mother's cage, they can be kept in a communal habitat until their first shed.

Keep the "nursery" simple, with a paper substrate and crumpled paper for hiding. Provide at least one large, but shallow water dish. This will help increase the humidity, but because it is shallow, will not serve as a drowning hazard for the young.

As the young shed their skin for the first time, they should be moved to their own cages. Provide typical husbandry for the small boas.

Begin feeding trials soon after their first shed. Many boas may refuse food the first or second attempt, so patience is required. By contrast, others will feed with little pause at the first opportunity.

This outrageous looking snake displays both the albino and hypomelanistic genes.

Chapter 13: Selected Subspecies Accounts

Chapter 13: Selected Subspecies Accounts

Despite the fact that most boas are relatively similar, there is considerable variation between the various subspecies – primarily as it relates to their color, pattern, size and temperament. Research the various subspecies and forms before deciding which boa is right for you.

1) Common Boas (*Boa constrictor imperator*)

Common boas are aptly named – the vast majority of boa constrictors in captivity belong to this subspecies. Pet stores and retailers, often mislabel these snakes, and call them "Columbian red-tail boas." While there are red-tail boas in Columbia, few are imported. Instead, most common boas hail from Central America.

Common boas may have red-colored tails, but the majority have brown or rust-colored tails. Common boas usually have relatively wide dorsal saddles that lack the "widow's peaks" that are often present on the saddles of *Boa constrictor constrictors*. Common boas generally have more than 22 dorsal blotches between the head and the vent.

Common boas are very hardy animals that are well suited for beginning snake hobbyists. They often become quite tame, but some South American populations of *imperator* are among the largest boas.

Currently, many snake keepers have placed more emphasis on the locality from which their common boa hails. For instance, a breeder interested in producing geographically "pure" offspring is unlikely to pair a common boa from Panama with a common boa from Honduras.

Chapter 13: Selected Subspecies Accounts

Most of the color mutations known in boa constrictors originated in this subspecies.

2) Red-tailed Boas (*Boa constrictor constrictor*)

Often called "true" red-tailed boas, boas of this subspecies often – but not always -- bear bright red or maroon tails. In some individuals and populations, the tail is almost purple.

Red-tailed boas are found throughout the northern portions of South America, and they may interbreed with common boas where their ranges meet.

Because they have evolved in slightly different habitats, with different selective pressures, considerable variation exists between red-tailed boas from different areas. Specimens from different ends of the subspecies' range may differ markedly.

Many hobbyists are particularly fond of specimens whose ancestors originated from Guyana or Suriname. These animals often feature a handsome grey ground color, though it normally becomes brown with age.

Additionally, boas from Suriname and Guyana often feature saddles that have "widow's peaks" or resemble the silhouettes of bats, although this is not a blanket rule. In general, the patterns of red-tailed boas are often more elegant than the blockier saddles of common boas.

The size of red-tailed boas varies with their location. Some of the largest boas known are red-tailed boas from east Peru. Conversely, female Suriname boas seldom exceed 10 feet in length.

From a husbandry standpoint, it is important to understand that red-tailed boas are somewhat more challenging than common boas are. Whereas common boas often endure the indignities of captivity and the learning curve associated with new keepers, red-tailed boas have narrower tolerances.

Chapter 13: Selected Subspecies Accounts

Red-tailed boas are shyer than common boas are. They are more likely to show signs of stress if they do not have access to suitable hiding places. Many true red-tailed boas, particularly those from Suriname and Guyana, do not tolerate handling as well as other subspecies do.

Some keepers recommend keeping red-tailed boas at slightly higher temperatures than common boas, but it is not yet clear that this is necessary. However, it is quite clear that they require slightly higher humidity than their common cousins do.

Red-tailed boas often fall victim to something called "regurgitation syndrome," in which they fail to digest food properly. This is usually caused by improper environmental conditions, high stress levels (such as occurs when they are handled too frequently) and aggressive feeding schedules.

Red-tailed boas should be fed less frequently than common boas, and the prey should be relatively small.

3) Argentine Boas (Boa constrictor occidentalis)

Argentine boas live further south than any other boa constrictor subspecies does. Accordingly, their habitat preferences and body color are somewhat different from those of common or red-tailed boas.

Argentine boas are very dark animals (which may be an adaptation that allows them to thermoregulate more effectively in the cooler climate). Some are nearly black, though others are dark brown.

While still present, their saddles are not as bold as those of boas with lighter ground colors are. However, the light spots within the saddles are very bold and quite striking.

Because their populations are decreasing in the wild, Argentine boas are listed on Appendix I of the Convention on International Trade of Endangered Species. Wild-caught animals are not available.

Chapter 13: Selected Subspecies Accounts

4) Long-tailed Boa (Boa constrictor longicauda)

The long-tailed boa is a beautiful and rare subspecies, not often seen in pet stores. The long-tailed boa's claim to fame is the color pattern. Long-tailed boas often display a yellowish-gray ground color, on top of which sit bold, black saddles. Their saddles are often simpler shapes than those of other subspecies, although they may be wider than those of red-tailed boas.

Long-tailed boas have the boldest facial markings of any boa subspecies. The line on the top of their heads is very bold and wide, and they possess very bold stripes behind their eyes. The tail of long-tailed boas is quite dark in color.

Some authorities suggest that long-tailed boas are simply a local color variety of Peruvian boas (Boa constrictor constrictor). The true nature of their relationship is not yet clear.

5) Hog Island Boas (*Boa constrictor imperator*)

The boas hailing from Cayo de los Cochinos (a group of small islands off the east coast of Honduras) possess a number of unique traits. Although they are regarded as the same subspecies that their mainland cousins are, most keepers and breeders agree that the form is very unique.

They were first discovered and imported to the United States and Europe in the mid-1980s. However, the demand soon outstripped the supply, and by the early 1990s, they had virtually disappeared from the island. Fortunately, protections were put into place, and the snakes have rebounded on the island.

A few lines of these boas, which became known by the name "Hog Island Boas," based on a loose translation of the island's Spanish name, became established. However, these desirable snakes are no longer as easily found as they were in the past.

Chapter 13: Selected Subspecies Accounts

A beautiful example of a Hog Island boa.

Hog Island boas are a small form; the largest females rarely exceed 6-feet in length, and most are smaller than this. Males may not exceed 5-feet in length. The combination of their small size and generally calm demeanor is enough to make the snakes popular; but their most attractive feature is likely their color.

While their basic pattern is similar to other common boas, Hog Island boas have yellowish ground colors and very light brown saddles. Their tail is often orange.

This super-light coloration is popular among many boa enthusiasts, but the most interesting thing is that these snakes change color over the course of the day. During the morning, the snakes are very pale, and the pattern can barely be distinguished. By the time night approaches, the saddles contrast very sharply with the ground color, and the snakes look spectacular.

While not the only snakes capable of altering their color, few are capable of such impressive levels of color change.

6) "Dwarf" Boas

From time to time, boas are advertised as being a "dwarf" variety. While it is true that many boa populations (particularly those from islands) tend to be smaller than average, most purported

Chapter 13: Selected Subspecies Accounts

"dwarves" become large once living in captivity, and provided with a "typical" captive feeding schedule.

This is unfortunate for all parties involved, and retailers that engage in such deceitful tactics bear responsibility for the outcome of these lies.

Nevertheless, captives from a few populations do retain the small size of their wild-roaming ancestors, even when provided with typical feeding schedules. All are recognized as members of the *Boa constrictor imperator* subspecies, but some may eventually be elevated and become full subspecies themselves.

These dwarf races, which rarely exceed 6 feet in length include:

- Crawl Cay Boas
- Hog Island Boas
- Tarahumara Boas
- Tamaulipas Boas
- Corn Island Boas
- Roatan Island Boas
- Cay Caulker Boas
- Ambergris Cay Boas
- Honduran Boas
- El Salvador Boas

Many of these forms are very rare in captivity, and command high prices when they are available. Because it takes years to verify that a purported dwarf will not reach large sizes, it is very important to purchase dwarf boas from reputable breeders.

Chapter 14: Further Reading

Never stop learning more about your new pet's natural history and biology of captive care. Doing so will allow you to provide your new pet with the highest level of care possible.

Books

Bookstores and online book retailers often offer a treasure trove of information that will help your quest for knowledge. While books represent an additional cost involved in turtle care, you can consider it an investment in your pet's well-being. Your local library may also carry some books about tortoises, which you can borrow for no charge. University libraries are a great place for finding old, obscure or academically oriented books about tortoises. You may not be allowed to borrow these books if you are not a student, but you can view and read them at the library.

Herpetology: An Introductory Biology of Amphibians and Reptiles

By Laurie J. Vitt, Janalee P. Caldwell

Academic Press, 2013

Snakes: Their Care and Keeping

Lenny Flank

Howell Book House

Understanding Reptile Parasites: A Basic Manual for Herpetoculturists & Veterinarians

By Roger Klingenberg D.V.M.

Advanced Vivarium Systems, 1997

Chapter 14: Further Reading

Keeping Snakes: A Practical Guide to Caring for Unusual Pets

David Manning

Barron's Educational Series

The Art of Keeping Snakes: From the Experts at Advanced Vivarium Systems

Philippe De Vosjoli

Advanced Vivarium Systems

Snakes: Everything about Selection, Care, Nutrition, Diseases, Breeding, and Behavior

Richard D. Bartlett, Patricia Pope Bartlett

Barron's Educational Series

Infectious Diseases and Pathology of Reptiles: Color Atlas and Text

Elliott Jacobson

CRC Press

What's Wrong with My Snake?

John Rossi, Roxanne Rossi

BowTie Press

The Boa Constrictor Manual

Philippe de Vosjoli, Roger Klingenberg, Jeff Ronne

BowTie Press

The Complete Boa Constrictor: A Comprehensive Guide to the Care, Breeding, and Geographic Races

Vincent Russo

Chapter 14: Further Reading

E. C. O. Herpetological Publishing & Distribution

Boas and Pythons of the World

Mark O'Shea

New Holland Publishers

Boas: Everything about Acquisition, Care, Nutrition, Diseases, Breeding, and Behavior

Doug Wagner

Barron's Educational Series

The Snakes of Trinidad and Tobago

Hans E. A. Boos

Texas A&M University Press

Magazines

Reptiles Magazine

www.reptilesmagazine.com/

Covering reptiles commonly kept in captivity, kingsnakes are frequently featured in the magazine, and its online partner.

Practical Reptile Keeping

http://www.practicalreptilekeeping.co.uk/

Practical Reptile Keeping is a popular publication aimed at beginning and advanced hobbies. Topics include the care and maintenance of popular reptiles as well as information on wild reptiles.

Websites

With the explosion of the Internet, it is easier to find information about reptiles than it has ever been. However, this growth has caused an increase in the proliferation of both good information and bad information. While knowledgeable breeders, keepers and academics, operate some websites, others lack the same dedication and scientific rigor. Anyone can launch a website and say virtually anything they want about boa constrictors. Accordingly, as with all other research, consider the source of the information before making any husbandry decisions.

The Reptile Report

www.thereptilereport.com/

The Reptile Report is a news-aggregating website that accumulates interesting stories and features about reptiles from around the world.

Kingsnake.com

www.kingsnake.com

Started as a small website for gray-banded kingsnake enthusiasts, Kingsnake.com has become one of the largest reptile-oriented portals in the hobby. Includes classifieds, breeder directories, message forums and other resources.

The Vivarium and Aquarium News

www.vivariumnews.com/

The online version of the former publication, The Vivarium and Aquarium News provides in-depth coverage of different reptiles and amphibians in a captive and wild context.

Journals

Herpetologica

www.hljournals.org/

Published by The Herpetologists' League, Herpetologica, and its companion publication, Herpetological Monographs cover all aspects of reptile and amphibian research.

Chapter 14: Further Reading

Journal of Herpetology

www.ssarherps.org/

Produced by the Society for the Study of Reptiles and Amphibians, the Journal of Herpetology is a peer-reviewed publication covering a variety of reptile-related topics.

Copeia

www.asihcopeiaonline.org/

Copeia is published by the American Society of Icthyologists and Herpetologists. A peer-reviewed journal, Copeia covers all aspects of the biology of reptiles, amphibians and fish.

Nature

www.nature.com/

Although Nature covers all aspects of the natural world, there is plenty for snake enthusiasts.

Supplies

Big Apple Pet Supply

http://www.bigappleherp.com

Big Apple Pet Supply carries most common husbandry equipment, including heating devices, food dishes and supplements.

LLLReptile

http://www.lllreptile.com

LLL Reptile carries a wide variety of husbandry tools, heating devices, lighting products and more.

Doctors Foster and Smith

http://www.drsfostersmith.com

Chapter 14: Further Reading

Foster and Smith is a veterinarian-owned retailer that supplies husbandry-related items to pet keepers. Additionally, their website features a wealth of information about reptile keeping and Russian tortoises.

Support Organizations

The National Reptile & Amphibian Advisory Council

http://www.nraac.org/

The National Reptile & Amphibian Advisory Council seeks to educate the hobbyists, legislators and the public about reptile and amphibian related issues.

American Veterinary Medical Association

www.avma.org

The AVMA is a good place for Americans to turn if you are having trouble finding a suitable reptile veterinarian.

The World Veterinary Association

http://www.worldvet.org/

The World Veterinary Association is a good resource for finding suitable reptile veterinarians worldwide.

References

Arnold J. Sillman, J. L. (2001). Retinal photoreceptors and visual pigments in Boa constrictor imperator. *Comparative Physiology and Biology*.

Buning, T. d. (1983). Thresholds of infrared sensitive tectal neurons inPython reticulatus, Boa constrictor andAgkistrodon rhodostoma. *Journal of comparative physiology*.

Düring, M. v. (1974). The radiant heat receptor and other tissue receptors in the scales of the upper jaw of Boa constrictor. *Zeitschrift für Anatomie und Entwicklungsgeschichte*.

Eells, B. C. (1968). Thermal Aggregation in Boa constrictor. *Herpetologica*.

F. BRISCHOUX, L. P. (2010). Insights into the adaptive significance of vertical pupil shape in snakes. *Journal of Evolutionary Biology*.

Irene Romero-Nájera, A. D.-B. (2007). Distribution, abundance, and habitat use of introduced Boa constrictor threatening the native biota of Cozumel Island, Mexico. *Biodiversity and Conservation*.

Janzen, D. H. (1970). Altruism by Coatis in the Face of Predation by Boa constrictor. *Journal of Mammalogy*.

Jayne, G. B. (2010). Substrate diameter and compliance affect the gripping strategies and locomotor mode of climbing boa constrictors. *The Journal of Experimental Biology*.

John S. Quick, H. K. (2005). Recent Occurrence and Dietary Habits of Boa constrictor on Aruba, Dutch West Indies. *Journal of Herpetology*.

References

Margarita Chiaraviglio, M. B. (2003). Intrapopulation variation in life history traits of Boa constrictor occidentalis in Argentina. *Amphibia-Reptilia.*

Miguel Angel Martínez-Morales, A. D. (1999). Boa constrictor, an introduced predator threatening the endemic fauna on Cozumel Island, Mexico. *Biodiversity & Conservation.*

Moore, S. M. (1969). Thermoregulation in the Boa Constrictor Boa constrictor. *Herpetologica.*

Rossi, J. R. (2006). *What's Wrong with My Snake?* BowTie Press.

Warren Booth, D. H. (2010). Evidence for viable, non-clonal but fatherless Boa constrictors. *Biology Letters.*

Withgott, J. (2000). Taking a Bird's-Eye View…in the UV. *BioScience.*

Index

Achilles tendonitis, 137
Albinos, 110
anerythristic, 113, 114
Anorexia, 106
Aquariums, 46, 47
Arabesque, 112
Aspen, 63, 64, 65
Bleach, 77
Blizzard, 114
Breeding, 79, 128
cage, 38, 45, 46, 47, 48, 49, 50, 53, 54, 55, 56, 62, 63, 65, 102, 103, 104, 105, 106
Cayo de los Cochinos, 124
Cleaning, 75, 76
Copulation, 118
Cork Bark, 68
Cycling, 117
Cypress Mulch, 64, 66
Dimensions, 45
Feeding, 78, 85
Gender, 40, 79, 121
Ghost, 114
Glass cages, 46
Heat, 35, 36, 51, 52, 53, 54, 55, 62
Heating, 56
Homemade Cages, 49
Humidity, 87
husbandry, 130, 132
Husbandry, 90
Hypomelanistic, 111, 112
Lights, 59

mites, 47, 103, 104, 105, 106
Motley, 112
Mouth rot, 102, 107
Newspaper, 65, 69
online, 127
Orchid Bark, 64
Paper Towels, 65, 69
Paradigm, 114
Parturition, 119
Pine, 64, 65
plastic storage boxes, 48
Prey, 82, 83
probe, 16, 57, 58, 59, 80
Pulp Products, 65
regurgitation syndrome, 123
Rheostats, 57
Screen Cages, 49
Shedding, 78
Snow, 114
Snowglow, 114
Substrate, 65, 134
Sunglow, 114
Temperatures, 56
Thermostats, 57, 58, 59
Transport, 94, 96
veterinarian, 9, 36, 44, 49, 76, 77, 98, 99, 100, 101, 102, 103, 104, 106, 107, 132
veterinarian's, 49
Water, 35, 36
widow's peaks, 121, 122

Published by IMB Publishing 2015

Copyright and Trademarks. This publication is Copyright 2015 by IMB Publishing. All products, publications, software and services mentioned and recommended in this publication are protected by trademarks. In such instance, all trademarks & copyright belong to the respective owners. All rights reserved. No part of this book may be reproduced or transferred in any form or by any means, graphic, electronic, or mechanical, including photocopying, recording, taping, or by any information storage retrieval system, without the written permission of the author. Pictures used in this book are either royalty free pictures bought from stock-photo websites or have the source mentioned underneath the picture.

Disclaimer and Legal Notice. This product is not legal or medical advice and should not be interpreted in that manner. You need to do your own due-diligence to determine if the content of this product is right for you. The author and the affiliates of this product are not liable for any damages or losses associated with the content in this product. While every attempt has been made to verify the information shared in this publication, neither the author nor the affiliates assume any responsibility for errors, omissions or contrary interpretation of the subject matter herein. Any perceived slights to any specific person(s) or organization(s) are purely unintentional. We have no control over the nature, content and availability of the web sites listed in this book. The inclusion of any web site links does not necessarily imply a recommendation or endorse the views expressed within them. IMB Publishing takes no responsibility for, and will not be liable for, the websites being temporarily unavailable or being removed from the Internet. The accuracy and completeness of information provided herein and opinions stated herein are not guaranteed or warranted to produce any particular results, and the advice and strategies, contained herein may not be suitable for every individual. The author shall not be liable for any loss incurred as a consequence of the use and application, directly or indirectly, of any information presented in this work. This publication is designed to provide information in regard to the subject matter covered. The information included in this book has been compiled to give an overview of the subjects and detail some of the symptoms, treatments etc. that are available to canines with these conditions. It is not intended to give medical advice. For a firm diagnosis of your dog's condition, and for a treatment plan suitable for you, you should consult your veterinarian or consultant. The writer of this book and the publisher are not responsible for any damages or negative consequences following any of the treatments or methods highlighted in this book. Website links are for informational purposes only and should not be seen as a personal endorsement; the same applies to the products detailed in this book. The reader should also be aware that although the web links included were correct at the time of writing, they may become out of date in the future.

Made in United States
North Haven, CT
28 April 2024